Taking Care of
MOMMY

By, Paula Linden, R.D. and Susan Gross

Illustrated by Linda Ervine Meek
Chapter Limericks by Kati Larson

Mary Ellen Family Books/Doubleday
Garden City, New York

Abridged from pages 55, 36-7, 174-5, 155, 170, 61, 205-6 and 140 in *THE PARENT'S WHEN-NOT-TO-WORRY BOOK* by Barry B. Behrstock, M.D. with Richard Trubo, copyright © 1981, by Barry B. Behrstock, M.D., reprinted by permission of Harper & Row Publishers, Inc.

Excerpt from *AMY VANDERBILT'S COMPLETE BOOK OF ETIQUETTE: A GUIDE TO CONTEMPORARY LIVING.* by Amy Vanderbilt. Copyright © 1978 by Curtis B. Kellar and Lincoln G. Clark, Executors of the Estate of Amy Vanderbilt Kellar & Doubleday & Co., Inc. Copyright © 1952, 1954, 1955, 1956, 1958, 1963, 1967, 1972 by Curtis B. Kellar and Lincoln G. Clark, Executors of the Estate of Amy Vanderbilt Kellar. Reprinted by permission of Doubleday & Co., Inc.

Reprinted with permission from *MOTHERHOOD, YOUR FIRST 12 MONTHS* by Deborah Insel, copyright © 1982 by Acropolis Books Ltd., 2400 17th St., NW, Washington, DC 20009.

OUR BODIES, OURSELVES, copyright © 1971, 1973, 1976 by the Boston Women's Health Book Collective Inc., reprinted by permission of Simon & Schuster, Inc.

Excerpt from *WORKING MOTHERS* by Jean Curtis. Copyright © 1975, 1976 by Jean Curtis. Reprinted by permission of Doubleday & Co., Inc.

Excerpt from *MOTHERCARE* by Lyn Delliquadri and Kati Breckenridge. Copyright © by Lin Delliquadri and Kati Breckenridge. Reprinted by permission of J.P. Tarcher, Inc., and Houghton Mifflin Company.

Excerpt from *HOW TO BE A MOTHER AND A PERSON TOO* by Shirley Radl is used with the permission of Rawson, Wade Publishers, Inc. Copyright © 1979 Shirley Radl.

To our mothers, Dorothy and Kit
for giving us life and love;

To our children, Laurie, Lee and Jeffrey
for giving us the time to take care of ourselves, so
that we could better take care of them; and

To our husbands, Howard and Neil
for giving us the encouragement, the love and the
time to fulfill our dream.

To my Dad
for giving me the confidence, the will and the spirit
to always be a winner ... be it win, lose or draw.
—P.L.

Many thanks to the following people for their contribution and support:

Our mothers-in-law, Bernice and Jane, for sharing our sense of humor and for not taking our mother-in-law "ribbing" personally;

Bernard, Bernice, Eric and Gayla, for giving us their homes, their refrigerators and all their love;

JoAnne S. Adams, John Angelo, Rhonda Angelo, Amy Assemany, Mark Borkin, M.D. (our SUPERDOC), Pierrette Durocher, R.N., Allan S. Emery, M.D., Aubrey H. Ettenheimer,

Dea Farrah, M.S.W., James M. Feld, M.D., Nancy Ginsberg, Marci Grant, Steven Grant, M.D., Mary Grinko (for peace of mind and love), Cathy Guisewite,

Jeffrey Katz, Kati Larson, Chris Luckes, David Lurie, Linda Ervine Meek (for capturing our essence), Gwen Murphy, Judge Joseph J. Pernick, Ian Pesses, Jerome F. Rose, M.D.,

Eric Rosenthal, Jeffrey Ross, Stanley Sherman, M.D., Janice Sherman,

Dorothy Simon, Judith H. Trepeck, C.P.A., Norman Trepeck, C.P.A., Lynn Walters, Cindee Zabner,

and Gayla Zoghlin, M.D., for acting as the official TAKING CARE OF MOMMY sounding board and sharing her objective eye, her relentless enthusiasm and her beeper number with us.

A special thanks to Jonathon Lazear for sharing our belief in **Taking Care of Mommy.**

A special thanks to the following people for participating in the **Taking Care of Mommy** survey:

JoAnne S. Adams, Pamela Assemany, Beth Aviv, Gail Bason, Lana M. Berndt, Mary Sue Berry, Susan Bloom, Sue Blumberg, Bobbie Borkin, Debra S. Brash, Judy Brenner, Marilyn Bruce, Cathy Cantor, Marlene Stortz Carron, Linda A. Casazza, Mindy Cherney, Susan Christman, Michele Chulick, Mrs. Fleet H. Davies, Heather Annatoyn Dickson, Peggy Dion, Sharon Disher, Connie Dreyer, Pierrette Durocher, Beth Erman, Linda Etkin, Kim Evans, Vicki Feisel, Nancy Fenster, Marilyn Findley, Connie Finlayson, Jacqueline Finn, Cindee Fischel, Barbara Fortune, Connie Gallagher, Michele Lee Gallagher, Denise Geller, Theresa Genereux, S. Gershonowicz, Lindy Giammattei, Margie Ginsberg, Katherine Gismondi, Esther Gold, Beth Goldsmith, Diana Gorgi, Dottie Goulding, Marci Grant, Susan Borock Grant, Sydell Grant, Lori Greenberg, Paula Gross, Susan Gross, Janet M. Haas, JoAnn Harry, Elizabeth Hathaway, Cindy Hertel, Lana Hyer-Prasse, Myra Lane Juhnke, Andrea Lilly Kahn, Nanci Kantor, Judy Kaufman, Elizabeth Keller, Julie M. Korotkin, Marilyn Krall, Barbara Krasman, Marlene Krochmal, Marilyn E. Krupa, Kathleen Larkin, Jill Q. Laurich, Roberta A. Leidal, Marisue N. Lenihan, Shari Levin, Amy Lieberman, Karen Linden, Cyd Little, Leslie London, Susan Loss, Kay Lurie, Melissa Lurie, Anita Maceri, Kathie MacLachlan, Linda Macklin, Carolyn Marks, Geri Mattocks, Kathy Matty, Faye Mendelsohn, Patty Mulkiten, Monni Must, Charlene D. Navarre, JoAnne Nosan, Jane Nutter, Joan Opiele, Karen Oram, Denise Parr, Paula M. Petrosky, Fran Prainito, Machelle M. Prainito, Ann Prows, Libby Racke, Jane Radner, Marilyn Rankin, Debra Sue Restivo, Ann C. Richards, D.D.S., Kathleen Robinson, Debra Shapiro Rosenberg, Dianne Rosenberg, Laurie Rosenthal, Marta S. Rosenthal, Risha Rothberger, Cherry Runde, E. Michele Samson, Jane Redfield Schwartz, Ruth Schwartz, Betty Schwartz, Jacqueline Sefferman, Susan H. Servais, Janice Sherman, Bobbie Siegel, Lori Simon, Sue Simon, Judith Sirvio, Shirley A. Soltesz, Nancy Solway, JoAnne Sosniak, Andrea Stahl, Susan Stettner, Anne D. Stockman, Jill Stone, Kristine Sullivan, Marcy Sultan, Ilene Techner, Irene Thomson, Cherolee Trembath, M.D., Judith Trepeck, Catherine Vanneste, Pamela N. Vinocur, Debbi Weisberg, Ginny Moceri Wener, Beth Wexner, Linda Wolf, Cindee Zabner, Debbie Zager ... and the many Mommies who returned their surveys and wished to remain anonymous.

TABLE OF CONTENTS

TABLE OF CONTENTS *continued*

Taking Care of Mommy was conceived on a grey plaid sofa during a candid discussion between two best friends. One had just given birth to her second child and the other was expecting her first. Six hours and three coffee cakes later, the curtain had been lifted, not only on what really happens during childbirth ("Paula, what's all this hemorrhoid stuff for?"), but on everything that happens from that day forward ("Susie, I promise—if you can't find childcare, I'll watch the baby while you go back to work!").

And thus, the second-time Mommy reduced the anxiety of the first-time Mommy, inspiring the creation of this book, a guide to taking care of Mommy while Mommy is taking care of the baby.

It's packed with honest and relevant information for Mommy about Mommy and it's spiced with the sense of humor so crucial to surviving motherhood. First-time Mommies will gain the confidence of "second-timers". And second-time Mommies will find the solutions they may have missed the first-time around.

Taking Care of Mommy begins with pre-hospital, covers the birth of the baby and continues right through the rigors of caring for a newborn *and* Mommy. It provides helpful hints for changing your husband into a Daddy, your mother into a grandmother, and your home into a workplace.

Here's the plan to reduce your hips, your pop-in company, your wasted hours—and your anxiety.

When you feel out of control, unshowered in your nightgown at 6 P.M.—make sure you take the time for taking care of Mommy, too!

—Paula and Susie

While preparing the nest for her chicks
Mommy's good sense and judgment were nix,
Despite her credentials
She forgot the essentials
And the first meal at home was breadsticks.

The Mother Hubbard Cupboard Syndrome

How to avoid having bare cupboards after the baby's born.

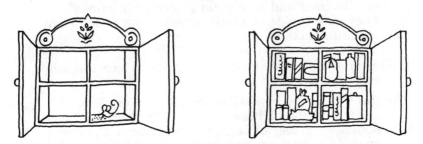

To use this chapter effectively, you must first determine how organized you are (or how organized your personality type allows you to be.) Circle the answers in the following test that best describes you. (No cheating, please!)

The "Mother Hubbard Cupboard Syndrome" Test

1. While taking a shower you decide that you want to wear your blue leather belt from two seasons ago. You ...

    a) know exactly where it is: in the triple dresser, third drawer on the left behind the red gloves.

    b) search the dresser, the attic and the closet. You find it hanging with the blue dress you wore to Aunt Freida's third wedding.

    c) checkout your entire bedroom, attic, basement, cleaners, best friend, two sisters-in-law ... and decide to wear your green suede belt instead.

2. Your newlywed girlfriend calls in a panic. She has invited her entire in-law family over for a special home-cooked meal. You offer your help by ...

    a) organizing her. You plan the entire six course menu, set her table, and make the Cherries Flambé.

    b) teaching here Rule Number One of having your mother-in-law for dinner: call the local cateress.

    c) calling her back with a wonderful recipe for Chicken Jubilee. Unfortunately, her dinner party was last Tuesday!

3. Your monthly checking account statement arrives with a note on it to call the bank. The first thing you do is ...

   a) check the statement against your register, only to find that they're in perfect balance. You call the bank, they wish you a "Merry Christmas" and tell you that the checks you reordered have arrived.

   b) panic. You pull yourself together, call the bank and find that your car loan has been approved.

   c) call the bank and wish them a "Merry Christmas". They wish you'd put a little money in your overdrawn checking account.

4. You show your husband how you'd like to have the baby's laundry done. The process takes you ...

   a) three days. You have a list describing every item and the detergent, bleach, laundry booster, and fabric softener you use for each. You describe every cycle in such detail that not only does he know how to operate the machine, but he now knows how to repair it.

   b) 20 minutes. You have him separate the whites from the darks and stick to the normal cycle.

   c) just long enough to point him to the laundry room.

5. You decide to serve a sour cream chocolate chip coffee cake for tomorrow night's poker game. You ...

   a) take out your three best sour cream chocolate chip coffee cake recipes to determine which one to use.

   b) preheat the oven, pull out the recipe, and call your neighbor to see if she has any chocolate chips.

   c) call your company and ask them to stop at the bakery and pick up a sour cream chocolate chip coffee cake on their way over.

6. You get a phone call from Margie Stonefield. It's been ten years since you've heard from her and you're all excited. She wants you to help plan your ten year class reunion. You tell her you're delighted to help and six months later ...

   a) you attend the reunion along with 93% of your class. The hall is perfectly decorated in blue and gold and the meatballs and chicken wings are delicious. Your class was right. You were, "The person most likely to plan the ten year class reunion!"

b) after attending 48 steering committee meetings, you show up the night of the reunion dressed in blue and gold, carrying the plate of brownies you promised to bake.

c) you're totally immersed in this project. It's the first time in your life that you've followed something through from beginning to end! The turn-out is great! Margie comes over to congratulate you ... you did a wonderful job of bringing together the wrong class.

7. It's spring. The tulips are blossoming, the birds are chirping, and the air smells fresh and clean. In order to enjoy your favorite season you must ...

a) do a thorough spring cleaning, including moving furniture, washing walls, and stripping floors. You arrange for additional help and get it all done in three weeks.

b) vacuum under the bed, dust the furniture, and clean out the refrigerator.

c) plan a trip.

8. It's Monday morning and your bathroom is "the pits". You ...

a) put on your pink rubber gloves, pick up the Lysol, Windex, chrome polish, plexi polish, four sponges, the toilet bowl scrubber, and emerge Tuesday evening.

b) pick up the Comet, paper toweling, and get to work.

c) shut the door.

9. It's time to go to the grocery store. You ...

a) make the trip alone, taking with you your coupon-coded shopping list (which you've organized according to the layout of the store), your Ronco food-clicking-tabulator, and your check-cashing card.

b) jot down a few of the things you know you need, and fill in as you go up and down the aisles. As the fish sticks move down the conveyor, you fish for your coupons.

c) wait until you are suddenly inspired as you drive past the market to go on a major shopping spree. Never mind that you have no list, no coupons (this week is "triple coupon"), and no money in your checking account (see question #3 above). 15 bags later you arrive home, only to find that you've forgotten the laundry detergent, the coffee, and the milk.

10. It's been a while since you've had your parents over for dinner. You call them up, set a date for Friday, and ...

a) plan your dinner menu considering taste, texture, and color. You include their favorite foods and top it off with a glazed, chocolate, Amaretto merinque cream torte.

b) wake up Friday morning, check out the 'fridge and freezer, and plan the menu accordingly.

c) "Hello, Mom. Could you stop at Harold's Pizzeria on your way over and pick up a large double-cheese pizza and a Greek salad?"

Scoring your Personality Type

7–10 A's: Type A:

Your biggest problem will be resisting the temptation to complete this chapter in your third month. You get "weak in the knees" when asked to organize a good committee or a messy closet. You're happiest when you have the time to set priorities and completely follow-through. You're filled with tenacity and self-control. (Perhaps that's why you turned in all those term papers the day after they were assigned in school!) Most Type A's never get the "nesting instinct", since they are forever nesting. But beware: you might get the sudden urge in your ninth month to rotate the tires or change the spark plugs.

7–10 B's: Type B:

You're the type that's practical enough to realize that this chapter has to be done, but smart enough to find the easiest and fastest way to do it. You're reliable and flexible—a great co-chairman for a Type A. You enjoy having your life organized and neat, but you don't stay up nights thinking about it. You pepper your daily chores with lists, but your life goes on if they're not followed. You have a few "A" tendencies and a few "C's". You're very well balanced.

7–10 C's: Type C:

This chapter is really for you! You are affectionately referred to as a "casual housekeeper". You tend to be creative and free-spirited. You're always volunteering for Type A's committee, though you rarely make it to the meetings. You don't believe in firm rules. (Perhaps that's why you turned in all those term papers the day after they were due in school!) You never use a list—you can't find it! And your husband is forever stopping on his way home for dog food and milk.

Now that you've established your personality "type", you can determine the best way to use this chapter. (Type A's will commit it to memory. Type B's will follow it. Type C's? Well, the fact that you are still with us is reassuring.)

Just as you wouldn't bake a cake without a recipe, you can't attempt to organize anything without a list. It's the key to all organization. So, buy a good notebook and keep it handy. (Attention Type C's: Don't lose it!)

This chapter is divided into two sections: Stocking Up (filling the cupboards) and Spring Cleaning (cleaning them). Use the lists provided as guidelines. Take one step at a time and, as with any overwhelming situation, you'll be in control.

Stocking Up
The case for the 58-bag shopping spree!

There will be enough to contemplate after you have a baby without worrying if there is enough soap, toilet paper, and salad dressing on hand. You can plan efficiently ahead of time by using the **Taking Care of Mommy** Theory of Supply and Demand:

Pay special attention to the items you use on a weekly basis (supply) and the quantities you use (demand). There are certain items that you'll never want to be without after the baby's born. Though these differ from Type A Mother (Lysol) to Type C (Oreos), the method for figuring them out is the same. Keep track in your notebook. (Type C's: Do you still have yours?)

Here's a grocery guide of supplies we recommend you have on hand. Use this as a checklist, making the necessary adjustments to fit your household. Try to build a two month stockpile.

(**TCOM Hint:** Fresh produce, dairy products and other perishables should be purchased by your family or friends before you come home from the hospital. Keep a list for them, too!)

8 Things Not To Buy When Stocking Up

1. Condoms, foams and jellies
2. Double-Bubble-Cream-Dream-Chocolate Cake
3. Mini pads
4. Hostess Twinkies and Ding-Dongs
5. The No. 1 Best Seller, **10,000 Things to do in your Spare Time**
6. Queen-size pantyhose
7. Maalox, Mylanta, Rolaids
8. Pickles and ice cream

TCOM Grocery Guide

Stockpiling the Cupboards

Staples
Coffee, tea, cocoa
Cereals
Pasta, rice
Oil, shortening
Flour
Sugar – granulated, brown
Crackers
Fruit and vegetables –
    canned, juices
Potatoes
Onions
Mayonnaise, salad dressings
Tuna fish, salmon, peanut
    butter
"Nibbles" for company: nuts,
    pretzels
Soups, bouillon
Jams, jellies
Gelatin: flavored, unflavored
Condiments, spices, catsup,
    mustard, etc.
Assorted baking needs:
    baking powder, vanilla, etc.

Paper Goods
Toweling
Toilet paper (lots & lots)
Tissues
Napkins, cups, plates
    (see "Etiquette")
Plastic wraps
Aluminum foil
Plastic bags for storage &
    freezing
Trash bags
Plastic freezer containers

Cleaning Supplies
Bleach: liquid and powdered
Laundry detergent
Fabric softeners
Dishwashing detergents
Dishwasher soap
Glass cleaner
Scouring cleaners, pads,
    polishes
Floor products
Disinfectants
Spray cleaner
Sponges, rubber gloves
Baby's laundry: special baby
    detergent & bleach

Stockpiling the Freezer
Butter
Bread
Potatoes
Juices
Vegetables and fruits
Hamburger patties, chicken
    parts, steaks, fish, etc.

Stockpiling the Vanity
Toothpaste, mouthwash
Tissues, toilet paper
Cotton swabs
Soap: hand, bath
Shampoo, conditioner
Deodorant
Cream: hand, face, body
Sanitary napkins

TCOM The Cooking Guide

Now that you've stocked the cupboards and freezer, you'll want to prepare a few household meals to have on hand after the baby's born.

Here are nine easy-to-fix-and-freeze meals, complete with cooking and freezing instructions. Make them in your ninth month. The recipes are simple and they're simply delicious. (Disclaimer for Type C's: The authors assume no responsibility for *your* substitutions.)

Everything here can be kept frozen for at least three months. However, we bet that at the end of six weeks your freezer will be bare!

Mrs. Quigley's Prize Meatloaf

Preheat oven: 325°   Cooking time: 1¼ hour

2 lbs. ground chuck
1 egg
½ cup bread crumbs
½ medium onion, grated
  or chopped
1 tsp. seasoned salt
½ tsp. pepper
½ tsp. garlic powder
½ can tomato soup

Topping:
½ can tomato soup
2 tbsp. mustard
2 tbsp. brown sugar

Mix all ingredients together, form into loaf pan and bake. After 45 minutes, spread topping and continue baking. Cool 10 minutes before slicing.

Freezing Instructions: Wrap well; freeze whole or in individual slices. (When freezing, undercook by 15 minutes to avoid drying out when reheated.)

Old Fashioned Beef Stew

Cooking time: 3–3½ hours

2 lbs. stewing beef, cubed
1 tsp. oil
¼ cup water
2 onions, cut in quarters
3 carrots, sliced
3 potatoes, cut in quarters

1 can whole tomatoes
  (15 oz.), including liquid
1 can corn, drained
1 10 oz. box frozen green
  beans
1 cup fresh or canned
  mushrooms (optional)

Braise meat, seasoned with salt, pepper, paprika, garlic and flour. Brown meat in oil with onions. Add tomatoes, water and simmer 2 hours. Add carrots and potatoes. Simmer for another hour. Add corn, green beans and mushrooms. Heat thoroughly and serve.

Freezing Instructions: Freeze in air-tight plastic containers.

Dotzy's Delicious Hawaiian Chicken

Preheat oven: 325°–350° Cooking time: 1 hour

Chicken—one fryer, quartered
Bread crumbs
Butter or oil

Sauce:
1-1½ cups pineapple juice

2 tbsp. cornstarch
½ cup white sugar
½ cup brown sugar
4 tbsp. vinegar
2 tbsp. soy sauce
dash salt

Bread chicken and brown in butter or oil. Combine sauce/ingredients and bring to boil. Pour sauce over chicken and bake 45 minutes, uncovered. Add 1 can pineapple chunks with juice and broil to brown.

Freezing Instructions: Freeze in air-tight plastic containers. Reheat in a 350° oven, covered for 30 minutes.

Woodland Ridge
Hearty Vegetable Soup

Cooking time: 4–5 hours

Split Pea Soup Mix—dry in
  package
½ cup dried split peas
½ cup barley
3 soup bones
1 lb. short ribs (cut in
  1″ pieces)
8 cups water
1 huge onion, quartered
½ tsp. garlic powder

1 small sweet potato,
  quartered
5 stalks celery, chopped
6 carrots, sliced
½ lb. fresh mushrooms,
  sliced
2 tsp. dry dill (fresh to taste)
1 tsp. salt to taste
½ tsp. pepper

Simmer for 4–5 hours; remove soup bones. Remove short ribs, discard fat & bones, and add lean meat back.

Freezing Instructions: Freeze in air-tight plastic container.

Scrumptious Spinach-Tuna Quiche

Preheat oven: 350° Cooking time: 45 minutes or
until golden brown

Combine and blend in blender
½ cup mayonnaise
2 tbsp. flour
2 eggs, beaten
½ cup milk

Add:
1-10 oz. package frozen
  chopped spinach,
  drained well
⅓ cup onions, chopped
8 oz. swiss cheese, grated

Pour into unbaked 9″ pastry shell and bake.

Freezing Instructions: Wrap tightly in aluminum foil. Underbake by 10-15 minutes, when freezing. Reheat covered in 350° oven after defrosting.

Isle Royal Barbeque Brisket

Preheat oven: 425° Cooking time: 5 hours

1 5 lb. brisket, seasoned well
   with salt, pepper,
   garlic powder, paprika
3 large onions, sliced in
   rings

5 potatoes peeled and
   seasoned to taste
1½ cups Open Pit Barbeque
   Sauce mixed with
2½ cups water

Brown brisket at 425° for 20 minutes on each side. Secure onions
on top (fatty side) with toothpicks; add barbeque sauce and water
and bake at 350° for 2 hours, uncovered, basting every 20 minutes.
Add potatoes, cover and cook for 1½ hours. Uncover for last 1½
hours, basting every 20 minutes. (Reheat at 325° for 1 hour before
serving; cover loosely with aluminum foil.)

Freezing Instructions: Freeze whole or slice in individual portions;
wrap well in plastic wrap and heavy foil. Freeze gravy and potatoes in
plastic air-tight container.

Jeffy's Favorite: Yummy-Macaroni-and-Cheese

Preheat oven: 350° Cooking time: 45 minutes

1-1¼ cups elbow macaroni
1 small onion
1 small red pepper
   (optional)
3 tbsp. butter or margarine
3 tbsp. all-purpose flour

2 cups milk
½ tsp. salt
dash pepper
2 cups shredded
   cheddar cheese
½ cup bread crumbs

Cook macaroni in boiling salted water until tender; drain. Melt butter;
blend in flour. Add milk. Cook and stir until thick. Saute onion and
pepper in butter. Add this mixture to the white sauce, along with
cheeses, salt and pepper. Mix until smooth. Combine sauce with
macaroni. Turn into 1½ quart casserole. Top with bread crumbs.
Bake until bubbly and brown.

Freezing Instructions: Allow to cool thoroughly; cut into serving
squares and individually wrap in plastic wrap and heavy foil. Freezes
up to four months.

Aunt Paulie's Special Chicken Soup

Cooking time: 3–3½ hours

1 large soup chicken,
   quartered and cleaned
   thoroughly
12 cups water
6 stalks celery, cut into thirds
6 carrots, sliced
1 large spanish onion,
   quartered

½ large sweet potato, cut
   in half
1 tsp. salt, plus more to taste
½ tsp. pepper, plus more
   to taste
fresh or dried dill to taste
   (optional)

Bring chicken to boil, skim off top. Turn to low, add remaining ingredients, cover and simmer for 3–3½ hours. Strain soup, reserving carrots. Return carrots to soup and refrigerate overnight. Skim off fat solidified on top.

Freezing Instructions: Freeze in air-tight plastic container. (Allow two inches at the top for expansion.)

(**TCOM Hint:** Use boiled chicken for chicken salad.)

Mary Alice's Luscious Lasagne

Preheat oven: 350°   Cooking time: 30–40 minutes

1 lb. ground chuck
1½ tbsp. oil
⅔ cup chopped onions
1 clove garlic, minced
¼ tsp. basil
½ tsp. salt
½ tsp. oregano
¼ tsp. black pepper
1 can tomatoes (1 lb.),
   including liquid

1 can tomato sauce (8 oz.)
½ cup grated Parmesan
   cheese
½ lb. lasagne noodles, 1½
   inch wide
¾ lb. Mozzarella cheese,
   thinly sliced
1 lb. cream-style cottage
   cheese

Saute onions and meat in oil until brown. Spoon-off excess fat. Add all seasonings, tomatoes and tomato sauce. Simmer covered for 30 minutes. Cool. Cook noodles according to package directions. Drain and cover with cold water.

Layer the bottom of a 13" x 9" x 2" baking dish with noodles. Add ⅓ of meat sauce on top. Add a layer of Mozzarella cheese, followed by a layer of the cottage cheese. Sprinkle with 3 tbsp. Parmesan cheese. Repeat twice ending with sauce and Parmesan cheese on top. Bake. Let stand 10 minutes before serving.

Freezing Instructions: Wrap well; freeze whole or in individual slices.

Little Known Facts on Freezing
1. Use quality foods to get the best frozen results. The freezing process cannot improve the quality of food – at best it retains it.
2. Cool cooked foods before freezing.
3. Wrap foods properly. Use special air-tight, moisture and vapor proof containers and heavy wraps, including: heavy-duty aluminum foil, heavy weight freezer bags, and Tupperware or the equivalent.
4. Freeze in portion sizes you will use without waste.
5. Label everything clearly with contents, dates and number of portions.

Spring Cleaning
No matter what time of the year

You are about to commit yourself to a thorough room-to-room spring cleaning. You don't, however, want to commit yourself to the hospital. So, get some help to make this task easier and safer.

It might seem like an arduous task now, but if you do your "spring cleaning" before the baby's arrival you'll return home to a house that's clean and fresh. And you won't have to worry about major house cleaning for many months to come.

Once again, organization is the key. Make a list of every room in your house and everything that needs to be done, including floor to ceiling, cleaning of drapes, carpets, windows, woodwork, fixtures, cupboards, and drawers.

(**TCOM Hint:** Special household work, like painting and wallpapering the nursery, should be scheduled during your eighth month. Allow plenty of time, since few workmen finish by the date promised.)

9 Ways to Fake Spring Cleaning
(Type C's: These are for you!)

1. Befriend a Type A and copy her notebook ... better yet, let her clean your house
2. Buy a big rug
3. Plant the oven
4. Spray "Mountain Pine" air freshener every 4 hours
5. Rearrange the furniture (Good decoy: focus on the furniture, not the dirt)
6. Padlock the dirty rooms
7. Find everything that's broken or needs fixing ... and hide it
8. Switch all the 150 watt light bulbs to 25 watts (Everything looks cleaner in the dark!)
9. Admit no one to your home wearing white

Congratulations! Your house is clean, your cupboards are stocked—you've avoided the Mother Hubbard Cupboard Syndrome. You've also mastered the basic concept of **Taking Care of Mommy**: getting organized! That wasn't so bad, was it?

> Type A's: "More! More!"
> Type B's: "It was o.k."
> Type C's: "You must be joking!?!"

It's time to prepare yourself for the days ahead. With organizational skills in hand turn the page ...

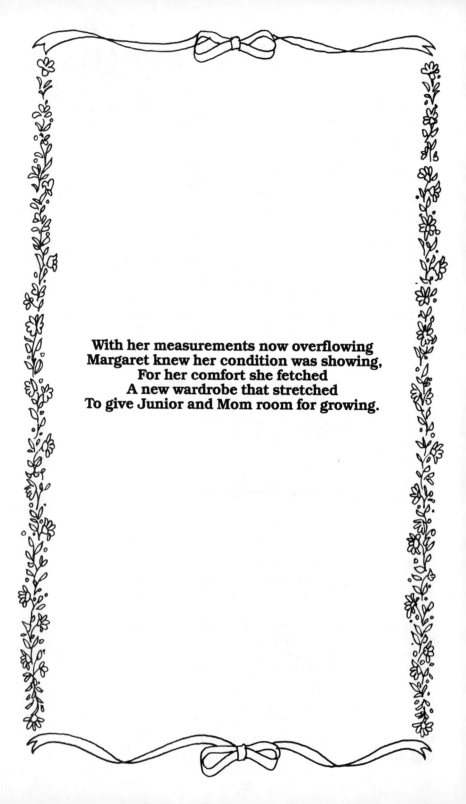

With her measurements now overflowing
Margaret knew her condition was showing,
For her comfort she fetched
A new wardrobe that stretched
To give Junior and Mom room for growing.

Mommy's Layette

Essentials for the New Mommy

It's a cold December morning. You wake up to 12 inches of freshly fallen snow. You jump into the shower and get ready for your seventh month check-up. (Dr. Horningridge will be so proud—you've only gained 11 pounds this month.) On your way out the door you stop to put on your favorite brown boots from last season, and 20 minutes later you ...

a) dry your tears, find your husband's ski boots in the front hall closet and make it to your appointment on time

b) cut out the instep and big toe of your favorite brown boots

c) call every size-9 friend you have to borrow a pair of bigger boots

d) change your appointment to 2:15, so you can stop at McGinney's shoe store on the way

To avoid feeling like Cinderella's fat stepsister, Mommy needs to take the time to prepare and pamper herself, too! So, put down your lists for the baby's layette and spend some time thinking about Mommy's layette ... the **Taking Care of Mommy** way.

Transitional Dressing: The Tight Squeeze

Many Mommies, especially first-time Mommies, are not ready physically and emotionally to wear their maternity clothes during their first trimester. However, they find themselves caught between their regular clothes, which are snug and uncomfortable, and maternity clothes, which are too big and awkward.

Here are some suggestions for surviving this difficult first stage of pregnancy—when you don't look pregnant, just fat!

The Navy Blazer Takes a Holiday
(New Basics for Mommy)

☐ pants and skirts with elastic waists

☐ wrap skirts

☐ loose fitting overtops

☐ regular clothes designed in the "one-size-fits-all" look

☐ dresses with tie belts

☐ jogging and exercise outfits with drawstring waists

These clothes will be terrific to wear after the baby is born, too. Psychologically, it's easier to wear transitional clothing, rather than maternity clothes, until you've lost all your weight.

Maternity Clothes: "The Sigh of Relief"
The Not-So-Subtle Signs of Needing Maternity Clothes

• Your briefs have become bikinis.

• You zip your favorite navy skirt half way up and hook it together at the top with a large safety pin.

• You've gone from 110 pounds to 140 pounds ... in two weeks!

• Your old college roommate congratulates you ... on finally gaining some weight.

• You've gone from an "inny" to an "outty".

• You have a 22 inch cleavage beginning at your chin and progressing down to your waist.

• You've popped ... your bra, your size-A pantyhose, and your favorite blue corduroys.

• You're wearing your husband's jeans and shirts ... because you look good in them.

• You have to reinforce your buttons after every meal.

Buy-laws for Maternity Dressing

#1: Buy-pass maternity clothes that don't make you feel good about yourself. (If you hated green plaids before you were pregnant, don't wear them now, just because your sister-in-law has a closet full.)

#2: Buy and large ... not extra-large, since maternity clothes are designed to grow with you. Don't buy them too big!

(**TCOM Hint:** Except for blue jeans, you will wear the same size in maternity clothes as you would normally wear, unless you've been celebrating the "rabbit's dying" at 31 Flavors.)

#3: Buyer beware of the saleswoman who exclaims, "That will look great worn belted later on." Don't even think about wearing maternity clothes after the baby is born! We have yet to meet a Mommy who a) doesn't wish she could burn her maternity clothes and b) doesn't find it very depressing to wear them afterwards.

#4: Wave buy-buy to thoughts of purchasing a lifetime supply. Even if you plan on having lots of children, styles change and it's fun to add a few new things to your maternity wardrobe with each pregnancy.

TCOM Survey Results

18% could fit into their regular clothes
0–4 weeks after delivery;
42% could fit 5–8 weeks after;
19% could fit 9–12 weeks after;
14% could fit 4–6 months after;
7% could fit 1 year or longer.

---

8 Things to Push
to the Back of Mommy's Closet the Day the Baby's Born

1. Your itsy-bitsy-teenie-weenie-yellow polka dot bikini

2. Your "Teddy" from Fredericks of Hollywood

3. Your cigarette-leg Jordache jeans

4. Your sultry, fire-engine red satin nightgown (Push it back, but not too far out of the way, since you'll want to pull it out in 4-8 weeks.)

5. Your green velour jogging suit (Check with your doctor—as much as you would like to work off those hips, you must wait for his "green light")

6. Your basic-black straight skirt with the slit up the front (Your shape is anything but!)

7. Your blue gingham-checked robe and your orange and white floral Hawaiian print housecoat (They're too easy to use as a crutch. Don't hide behind them.)

8. All of your maternity clothes. (They will fit, so don't depress yourself.)

Drip Dry!

This is not the time for Mommy to accumulate a wardrobe filled with cottons, linens, and silk—unless she is married to a dry cleaner. Stick with polyester or polyester blends (even though they may stick to you!). Easy-to-care fabrics are the best for Mommies, at least during pregnancy.

Feet First!

Since Mommy's feet often swell during pregnancy, she shouldn't attempt to stuff or cram them into shoes too small. Buy one or two pairs of shoes, one-half to one full size larger in a neutral color. Keep the heel low—pregnant women tend to be clumsy. (You will not look thinner wearing six inch heels. In fact, you'll look fatter lying flat on the floor after the fall!)

"Third Floor, Lingerie"

As your body grows in one direction, you will be stretching out your lingerie in the other. Ultimately, you will ruin mostly everything, since bras, underpants, and nightgowns will not snap back into shape like you will.

Therefore, you have two choices: you can buy new lingerie now (maternity) or you can wait and buy new lingerie later (a nice treat after the baby is born). Though the preference is strictly personal, **TCOM** suggests you purchase good support bras during pregnancy and comfortable, "one-size-fits-all" maternity underpants. (They're great to wear in the hospital after the baby is born, too!)

The ABC'S of Mommy's Layette
Tips on The Well-Planned Maternity Wardrobe
from Top to Bottom

A Accessories

In: jewelry, scarves, hats, perfume

Out: nothing, live it up!

B Bras

In: good support and proper fit

Out: going braless; pushing your chest up to your Adam's apple.

C Capes

In: buying one or borrowing one for maximum comfort

Out: renting one from Scary Larry's Costume Rentals.

D Dark hose

In: matching them to dark shoes in fall and winter for a slimmer look.

Out: matching them to white "spectators" in spring and summer.

E Elastic lines

In: never!

Out: tight bras, tight slips, tight panties, tight hose.

F Fancy clothing

In: keeping them simple; borrowing.

Out: stockpiling.

G Girdle

In: great support for Mommy's back.

Out: wearing it three years later.

H Hemlines

In: longer in front.

Out: longer in back.

I Intimate apparel

In: maxi or mini pads.

Out: tampons.

J Jumpers

In: all of them—they're Mommy's most flattering, comfortable look.

Out: forgetting to buy them in denim.

K	Knits	In:	if you're a size six or smaller.
		Out:	if you're a size ten or larger.
L	Layers	In:	taking them off.
		Out:	putting them on.
M	Make-up	In:	using it often; using it generously.
		Out:	using it theatrically.
N	Nightgowns	In:	cool and comfortable.
		Out:	warm and flannel.
O	Over-blouses	In:	wearing it long enough to cover panel on skirts and pants.
		Out:	wearing it on Wednesday with Tuesday's spaghetti stains.
P	Pants (jeans)	In:	when cut generously and flattering.
		Out:	when cut so tight Mommy can't sit down.
Q	Queen-size panty hose	In:	they're cheaper and more comfortable.
		Out:	hose that stop at Mommy's hips.
R	Regular blouses	In:	when unbottoned under jumpers.
		Out:	when unbuttoned over jeans.
S	Shoes	In:	low heels and wedges.
		Out:	high-fashion spikes and boots.
T	Tight clothing	In:	when you're built like "Charlie's Angels".
		Out:	when you're built like Charlie.
U	Underpants	In:	"one-size-fits-all".
		Out:	regular.
V	Ventilation	In:	cotton crotches
		Out:	polyester crotches

W Waisted belts	In:	first few months.
	Out:	last few months.
X X-tras	In:	maternity bathing suits.
	Out:	bikinis.
Y Youthful styles	In:	bright colors, calico prints, contemporary cuts.
	Out:	drab, dreary colors and matronly styles.
Z Zippers	In:	when they go all the way to the top.
	Out:	when they're short-stopped half way up.

Taking Care of Mommy in the Nursery

Every book ever written about motherhood details the baby's layette, including setting up the nursery for the baby. What's often forgotten, however, is how to make Mommy feel at home in the nursery, too:

The rocking chair must be comfortable! You might have to "try on" a lot of them before finding the one that fits you best. If you fall in love with a rocking chair that looks great, but you can't sit in it without tipping over, forget it! Also, back pads and cushions will make your hours of rocking more enjoyable.

(TCOM Hint: Keep an ottoman handy for long, middle of the night feedings.)

A lighted clock is great for late night feedings. Type A's will want to use it to note the exact duration of the 2 a.m. feeding. Type C's may not mind being left in the dark.

Hand cream for Mommy is a gentle touch for soothing dry hands after diaper changes and sponge baths.

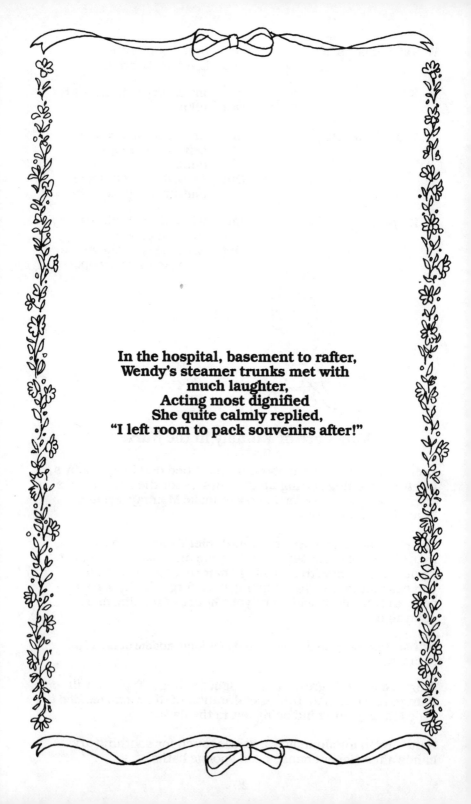

In the hospital, basement to rafter,
Wendy's steamer trunks met with
much laughter,
Acting most dignified
She quite calmly replied,
"I left room to pack souvenirs after!"

Packing Up

Yours. Mine. And Ours.

92% of the respondents to the **Taking Care of Mommy** survey indicated that when they packed for the hospital – they blew it! Some brought things they should have left at home, while others left at home things they should have brought.

Therefore, we present you with the **Taking Care of Mommy** Complete Packing Guide: how to fill, cram, stuff, and bag Mommy's head, body, and suitcases with everything from rolling pins to rolls of dimes.

So, grab your valises, trunks and totes – it's time to pack it up right! And on the "big day" if your "flustered Freddy" should leave you "holding the bag", at least you'll know it's packed correctly.

QUOTABLE TOTABLES
(Packing Mommy's Head)

Before you think about packing for the hospital, you'll want to pack your mind full of information that will help you during and after childbirth. Spend as much time as you can reading books before the baby's born (see recommendations at the end of this chapter), because free time will be at a premium afterwards.

Choosing The Hospital

One of the first things you'll want to do after you find out you're pregnant is choose the hospital for your baby's birth. Many doctors are affiliated with more than one hospital and may offer you a choice. Discuss the various options with your doctor and find out his preference. He may favor the labor nurses in one hospital and you may favor the birthing rooms in another.

You'll also want to think about the following: a) the location: how far away is it and how long will it take you to get there;

31

b) the facilities: birthing rooms, neonatal intensive care unit, educational classes; c) the policies: will they let you call your "best friend" from the recovery room (ours did!), what are the bonding and visitation rules; can siblings view birth; can Daddy view C-section; rooming in; d) take a tour and consult friends who've delivered at the hospitals you're considering.

10 Things to See on the Hospital Tour

1. Admitting
2. Maternity floor
3. Labor room
4. Delivery room
5. Recovery room
6. Birthing room
7. Newborn nursery
8. Cafeteria
9. A **real** newborn
10. Great Aunt Sara in 6-North Orthopedics (optional)

Childbirth Classes

Contact local hospitals, schools, universities, and the American Red Cross to find out the classes available in your community. Enroll in a good childbirth class. Also consider taking a first aid and/or baby care class.

Choosing a Childbirth Class
(7 Steps to Breathing Easier)

1. Size — The smaller, the better (no more than 12 couples)

2. Price — Make sure you're getting your money's worth; comparative shop.

3. Duration — 6–8 weeks; 2 hours per class.

4. Content — Sufficient information, discussion, and practice time to master the techniques for both you and your coach.

5. Support — Discussion of the emotional aspects of labor, breast feeding, and parenting.

6. Location — How far is the class from your home?

7. Instructor — Qualifications, experience, and references.

Potable Totables
(Packing the Tummies)

Mommy: Good nutrition should begin well before conception and continue through your entire pregnancy. However, at the end of your ninth month your exhaustion may cause you to become lazy about your eating habits. You're overweight, overdue, and over-indulging in chocolate chip cookies and butter pecan ice cream. You don't have the energy to prepare or the appetite to eat a full, eight course home-cooked meal. You're not alone.

Remember, since delivery is a very strenuous time, it's vital that you eat healthy foods, filled with proteins, vitamins, and minerals. While this advice is tough to follow, try to force yourself to eat balanced meals with a lot of protein-rich foods. Be sure to keep the meals small and pack your tummy with the "Basic Four".

Daddy: It's in everybody's best interest to keep Daddy's tummy filled with energy-packed foods during labor. Be sure to pack a special bag for Daddy's trip to the hospital, too!

The Labor Room Spread

Bologna & Swiss on Rye (heavy on the mustard)

Gatorade (gallon jug, two straws)

Apple (peeled, cored, and dipped in lemon to prevent browning)

Raisins (golden, seedless)

Kit Kat (frozen to prevent melting)

Dr. Brown's Cream Soda (cold, in flip-top can)

Napkin (dinner size)

Toothpick (blue or green frill on top)

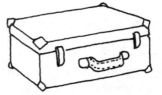

Notable Totables
(Packing Mommy's Suitcase)

3–5 nightgowns/1 robe/slippers

(If nursing, make sure you have front openings; the length of the gowns are subject to personal preference; slippers – **not** furry)

(**TCOM Hint:** Use hospital gowns whenever you are not seeing guests and at night. They are more comfortable and the hospital does the laundry!)

6–8 pairs underpants
(maternity underwear will be most comfortable)

2–3 regular size bras to help bind you if you are not nursing or 2-3 nursing bras if you are nursing

1 outfit for homecoming

(don't depress yourself: make sure it's a maternity dress – you can always belt it!)

Stationery, envelopes, stamps, birth announcements, address book with phone numbers, magazines, a good book.

Toothpaste, toothbrush (most hospitals provide you with a set, but it is still nice to have your own), soap, perfume, manicure supplies, shampoo, comb, brush, hair blower/curlers.

8 Things NOT to Pack

The family jewels	Sanitary belts and pads
Purse, wallet and keys	Silk peignoir sets
Size six Calvin Klein jeans	Chocolate chip cookies and Hershey Kisses
Alarm clock with snooze control	Mother/Mother-in-law

Packing the Lamaze Bag

Keep this separate from your suitcase and take it with you in the labor room

*pre-registration forms
*chapstick
*lollipops
tennis balls
ice packs
brown paper bag

towels
pillows
focal point (picture or item
    used for concentration
    point)
rolling pin

*important

Gloatable Totables
(Daddy's Call List)

It's extremely important to assemble your call list before the baby is born, so that friends and family are not forgotten in the excitement. Put it together in your eighth month in order of importance. (Your grandmother would be devastated if she heard the news from the butcher.)

Be sure to include both business and home phone numbers, complete with area codes. (Don't assume Daddy will remember phone numbers—he'll have a hard enough time just remembering his name.) Also, list the pediatrician and any clergy you need to notify.

Set aside a roll of dimes and keep it with the list, unless you bought your own wireless phone for the occasion.

(**TCOM Hint:** A phone company credit card may also be helpful and it is a free service for Mommy and Daddy.)

The "You'll-Want-To-Tell-The-World— But-You-Should-Resist Calling" List

☐ Daddy's ex-wife

☐ Mommy's fifth grade teacher, Mrs. Bloom

☐ Mommy's Great Uncle Charlie in China

☐ Daddy's barber, Mr. Phyllis

☐ Vito, the fruit man

☐ Anyone out of order on your list

35

Dotable Totables
(Packing for the Baby)

(**TCOM Hint:** Place all of baby's items in a separate bag for Daddy to bring to hospital.)

Many Mommies can't pack for the baby without rubbing a rabbit's foot and throwing a chicken bone over their left shoulder. If you feel these urges and are now searching for your lucky charm, then simply leave this list for Daddy to follow after the baby is born.

Innerwear

(**TCOM Hint:** Have plenty of supplies while waiting to be discharged: hospitals are notoriously slow at releasing new Mommies and babies.)

2 Undershirts

(In case the baby wets or spits on the first one before you actually get to leave.)

2–3 Newborn diapers

(The hospital will provide you with diapers, but if you prefer elastic legs to prevent leaking, pack your own.)

Homecoming Outfit

1) Gorgeous, hand-knit creation that buttons up the back and was lovingly made by Great Aunt Lilly just for the trip home. The baby will look adorable, but who will see her?

2) A sensible terry sleeper. The baby will look adorable in this practical outfit and she can go directly to her crib without changing.

Outerwear

Winter: sweater, warm bunting and/or heavy blanket

Spring/Fall: sweater, light weight bunting and/or medium weight blanket

Summer: If very hot, sleeper and light weight receiving blanket

(Remember: most doctors recommend that you use Mommy's bodily thermostat as a guide to keeping your baby comfortable.)

Formula—for non-breast fed babies (The hospital will provide you with formula for the ride home, plus a starter kit, which will last 24—48 hours.)

Car Seat—safety tested and approved; hooked up and ready for the baby. (Use it on the ride home from the hospital. Remember: most accidents occur within 25 miles from home.)

And, finally...

Packing the Diaper Bag

Imagine...

You're having a relaxing afternoon outing with your mother and your two month old son. Suddenly, as you're strolling through the mall, your eyes start to water and your mother passes out. You look down at little Georgie in his stroller... and gasp! His bodily clock went off three hours early.

Nothing frustrates a new Mommy more than not having the things she needs when she's out with the baby. It's embarrassing and demoralizing!

The diaper bag is Mommy's most important bag. It's the only one you'll pack in April and unpack in September...two years later.

So, take the time to anticipate your needs and adequately pack your diaper bag. Be sure to keep it stocked. Don't assume that your 82 year old grandmother keeps a box of diapers (newborn size, that is) in the pantry or that Aunt Selma has strained apple juice on hand.

Here's the **Taking Care of Mommy** guideline for packing the perfect diaper bag...the bag that takes care of baby and Mommy, too.

The TCOM Diaper Bag

(**TCOM Hint:** Shoulder bags are best because they leave Mommy with two free hands.)

For Baby	**For Mommy**
4–5 disposable diapers	Aspirin
Extra undershirt and sleeper	Hand cream (Hands get dry when constantly changing diapers)
Wipes	
Petroleum jelly	Spot remover (Great for removing spit up, or worse, from Mommy's clothes)
Bags with ties for dirty diapers (Recommended: Hefty scrap bags)	
	Lipstick and other make up
Extra bottle of formula, water and/or juice	Extra keys for car and house (You'll be locked out of both more times than you care to count)
Extra nipples	
Receiving blanket, rattle, bib	Extra pantyhose (Babies love pulling at Mommy's legs)
	Earplugs (Helps on difficult ride home)

Recommended Reading List

Childbirth Books:

Bean, Constance A.
Methods of Childbirth New York: Doubleday, 1974

Lamaze, Fernand
Painless Childbirth: The Lamaze Method
New York: Pocket Books, 1972

Nursing:

Carson, Mary
The Womanly Art of Breastfeeding Franklin
Park, Ill.: La Leche League International,* 1963

*non-profit international organization set up to support and inform women interested in breastfeeding baby.

Pryor, Karen
Nursing Your Baby New York: Pocket Books, 1973

Pregnancy:

Ingelman-Sundberg, Axel, Wirsen, with pictures by Nilsson
A Child is Born New York: Dell, 1966
(unique photos of fetal development)

Fleming, Alice
Nine Months New York: Harper & Row, 1972
(a good description of pregnancy)

Childcare:

Brazelton, T. Berry
Infants and Mothers New York: Delacorte, 1969
Caplan, Frank, The Princeton Center for Infancy and
Early Childhood
The First Twelve Months New York: Bantum Books, 1978
(Excellent overview of every month—all developmental
skills—physical—emotional—wonderful reference)

Spock, Benjamin
Baby and Child Care
(Great for comfort and emergency aid)

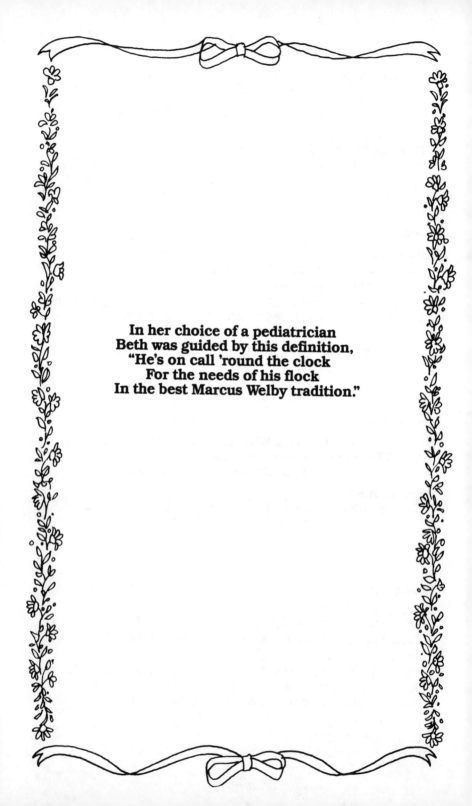

In her choice of a pediatrician
Beth was guided by this definition,
"He's on call 'round the clock
For the needs of his flock
In the best Marcus Welby tradition."

*Superdoc

Baby, have we got a Doc for you!

There are as many guidelines to selecting a good pediatrician for your baby as there are pediatricians. However, here is a special checklist of the credentials a pediatrician should have to meet *your needs*...for "taking care of Mommy", too.

You know you've chosen the right pediatrician if...

You feel comfortable with him. Your child's doctor (pediatrician) will provide you with medical and psychological guidance, education, and support for a long, long time. If you can't speak to him about the color of Johnny's last bowel movement without turning a similar color, you need a switch. Motherhood is filled with seemingly awkward problems. A good pediatrician will keep your anxiety level low and keep you prepared for each bend of the road.

He listens to you. New mothers, as a matter of fact, all mothers, ask a lot of questions. And they're not silly. You shouldn't be made to feel intimidated or inadequate by asking them. *You have the right to be informed about any and all decisions your pediatrician makes concerning your child.* You must be able to communicate openly and honestly. If you find him more involved with the mural on the wall than with your questions, you've probably missed the boat. Move on to the next "peer".

You understand his explanations. You should understand him when he speaks and understand what he is saying. If he speaks clearly and simply and doesn't have the need to impress you with medical jargon, you've found the right doctor!

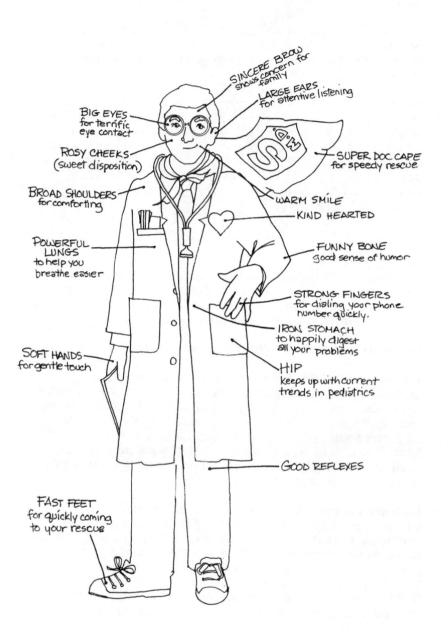

SINCERE BROW
shows concern for family

LARGE EARS
for attentive listening

BIG EYES
for terrific
eye contact

SUPER DOC CAPE
for speedy rescue

ROSY CHEEKS
(sweet disposition)

BROAD SHOULDERS
for comforting

WARM SMILE

KIND HEARTED

POWERFUL
LUNGS
to help you
breathe easier

FUNNY BONE
good sense of humor

STRONG FINGERS
for dialing your phone
number quickly.

IRON STOMACH
to happily digest
all your problems

SOFT HANDS
for gentle touch

HIP
keeps up with current
trends in pediatrics

GOOD REFLEXES

FAST FEET
for quickly coming
to your rescue

He comes highly recommended ... from friends, your obstetrician, the Department of Pediatrics at your community hospital or medical school, or the *Directory of Medical Specialists*. His office walls display the necessary academic credentials, along with Aunt Martha's needlepoint. Make certain he's board (not bored) certified!

His office schedule suits your needs. Is he a sole practitioner or is he affiliated with a group practice? (If he is one-out-of-seven, is your appointment with him honored or does the office staff play "pediatric musical chairs"?) What is his call schedule? Who covers for him on evenings, weekends, and days off? (You can't expect your pediatrician to always be at your beck and call, but if you really need him, will he be available?)

A happy relationship with your pediatrician can make a tremendous difference in your self-confidence as a Mommy and the pleasure you derive from your baby. Take time to find and interview your pediatrician before the baby arrives, so that you and your "new bundle of joy" can rest easily.

You trust his judgment. This is the part where your brain (he's got the proper medical credentials) gets together with your gut (Mommy's intuition). Some mothers are comforted by knowing their doctor's gray hair reflects years of practical experience, while others find reassurance in the contemporary medical knowledge of a young doctor, fresh out of his residency. Whether you prefer the "Geritol" or the "Clearasil" set, or someone in between, it's important that you feel absolutely sure about your doctor and his ability.

You like him a lot! He's a kind, compassionate human being.

---

*The term "Superdoc" and the reference through this chapter to the pediatrician as "he" is intended to embody both male and *female* pediatricians.

The Bonus Test
(Little extras for Mommy)

You know you've really chosen the right pediatrician if . . .

1. (2 pts. each) The office waiting room has: __ a sick baby side __ a well baby side __ plenty of room __ plenty of chairs for big people as well as little people (+10 pts. if coffee and cake are served.)

2. (5 pts.) There are more than three toys/books to play with that aren't broken or ripped. (+5 pts. if there are toys/books in the examining room; +5 pts. if there is reading material for Mommy, i.e. *Parents, McCalls,* etc.)

3. (5 pts.) The office takes Visa and Mastercard. (+5 pts. if they will bill you through the mail; +25 pts. if there's a "club plan": pay for 9 visits, get 10th visit free.)

4. (2 pts. each) He gives free samples of: __ vitamins; __ formula; __ medicine; __ disposable diapers; __ sugar water (+75 pts. if he gives out free samples of Chanel, Estee Lauder, or Mommy's favorite scent.)

5. (10 pts.) He makes house calls. (+150 pts. if he'll stop to pick up groceries on the way.)

6. (3 pts.) He has nice nurses. (−5 pts. for each nurse who snarls.)

7. (5 pts.) He remembers your name and your child's name when he walks into the room. (−50 pts. if the name he remembers is wrong; −100 pts. if he can't remember his own name.)

8. (3 pts.) He distributes growth charts and relevant reprints from medical journals. (+10 pts. if he distributes reprints from *Bon Appetit* or *Gourmet;* −25 pts. if his wife is there selling her baked goods.)

9. (10 pts.) He calls the next day to follow-up on your sick child. (+40 pts. if he send flowers.)

10. (3 pts.) He takes you on time for your appointment. (+10 pts. if he's early; −50 pts. if he's waiting for you in the elevator.)

11. (5 pts.) He takes time to ask questions about poison control, car seats, child proofing. (+10 pts. if he really wants to know how you are; −75 pts. if he really doesn't give a −.)

12. (3 pts.) He has good parking. (+10 pts. if valet; −50 pts. if the doctor is the car parker.)

13. (3 pts.) He has weekly evening office hours. (+25 pts. if he's open on Sundays; +100 pts. if he serves dinner.)

14. (2 pts.) He saves you money by writing the prescription in the generic name. (−25 pts. if he tacks on the savings to his fees.)

15. (3 pts.) His patient rooms are cutely decorated with mobiles, murals or pictures. (+10 pts. if there's a bulletin board with pictures of *all* his patients; −30 pts. if your son's picture is the only one on the board.)

16. (2 pts.) There is a pharmacy in the building. (+10 pts. if it is a discount pharmacy.)

17. (2 pts.) There is a cafeteria in the building. (+15 pts. if they will "hold the pickles, hold the lettuce.")

18. (2 pts. each) He provides waiting room entertainment: __ fish tank (+20 pts. if live fish show) __ television set __ "Sesame Street" or educational video recordings. (+20 pts. if video recording of your favorite soap opera are provided.)

19. (3 pts.) He gives children sugarless candy and gum. (−10 pts. if he gives lollipops; +10 pts. if he has Godiva chocolates for you.)

20. (10 pts.) He returns your phone calls quickly. (+25 pts. if he calls you back within the hour; +50 pts. if your number is on his automatic dialer.)

Scoring

100 or above: Wonderdoc. What a wonder-ful doctor you've found, though we can't help wonder-ing if he's a) your parent; b) your spouse; c) your best friend. If that's not the case, then we wonder if you'd mind having him contact us (or better still the *Guinness Book of Records.*) If he's as capable as he is clever, he is truly the 9th Wonder of the World.

85–99: Superdoc. He's our hero. This mild mannered practitioner gives you old fashioned dedication and creature comforts. He is wise, considerate, and compassionate. He doesn't have to leap tall buildings to impress you—you'll find him flying to your aid in times of need.

70–85: Dr. Strangelove: Though his office may have a strange setting, his patients love him. They flock to him because he's a good doctor. You may not be comfortable while you're waiting to see him, but you're comforted by his knowledge and gentle manner.

Below 70: **"What's Up Doc?** Did you forget about Mommy? Though this pediatrician may excel at taking care of your child, he's failed at taking care of you. (Rx: Send him a copy of this chapter and a fish tank for Christmas!)

You know you've chosen the wrong pediatrician if . . .

1. His office offers S&H Green Stamps and a free turkey on the first Monday of the month.

2. The waiting room is always empty.

3. He needs to consult the medical journal when your child asks, "How did Horton hatch the egg?"

4. When chitchatting he casually mentions that he hates kids.

5. He thinks the "RH Factor" is a new science fiction movie.

6. He enters the examining room with his stethescope in one hand and golf clubs in the other.

7. The only "Spock" he's familiar with is on the U.S.S. Enterprise.

8. When paying your bill, you are asked to make the check out directly to the Cadillac dealership.

9. His idea of a long weekend off is "going South for the winter".

10. He thinks "Roseola" is a new summertime drink.

The Ten Most Common Questions
Mommy Asks the Doctor
(A survey of ten pediatricians)

1. "How many times daily should I change Johnny's diaper?"; "What should I use when changing a diaper?"

2. "Is Johnny really beautiful or am I prejudiced?"

3. "Should I breast feed or bottle feed?"

4. "I think my baby isn't pooping enough"; "I think my baby is pooping too much".

5. "Is Johnny's penis the proper size?"

6. "When will Amy sleep though the night?"

7. "Is Sara teething?"

8. "When should I add solid foods?"

9. "I think my baby has colic ... HELP!"

10. "Is Georgie too fat ... or just too short?"

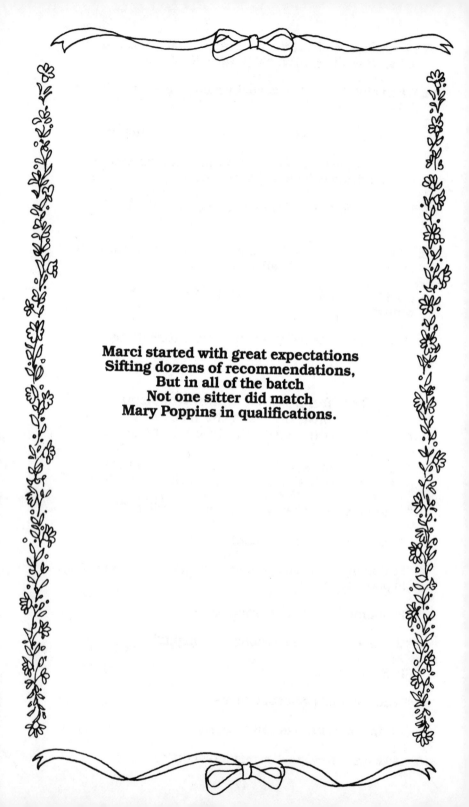

Marci started with great expectations
Sifting dozens of recommendations,
But in all of the batch
Not one sitter did match
Mary Poppins in qualifications.

Help, Help!

Coming to Mommy's Rescue

Help

Nary a Mommy can function every hour of every day without being rescued by her husband, mother, or hired helper. While "help" comes in many forms, we have devoted this section to the most popular help utilized by Mommies today: the baby nurse, the housekeeper, and the babysitter.

Here are some suggestions for finding qualified people who will excel at taking care of Mommy.

Mommy's Baby Nurse

The 5 Warning Signs of a Bad Baby Nurse

1. *She* sleeps through the 2:00 A.M. feeding.

2. The "soap" she recommends is "General Hospital".

3. Her parole officer calls.

4. She pockets your great grandmother's silver tea set as a "little souvenir" of her stay.

5. She's miraculously managed to contain your baby's diaper rash to your husband, three kids, and the dog.

A baby nurse is hired to live in Mommy's home for a predetermined time period, (usually one, two, or three weeks) to care for the baby while Mommy is recuperating from delivery. The baby nurses's qualifications range from years of practical experience to certification as a licensed practical nurse (LPN). This is a wonderful luxury, if Mommy is lucky enough to afford it.

While many baby nurses will care for Mommy's needs, too, you cannot expect the nurse to run your errands, clean your house or cook your meals. You can expect her to take total

49

charge of the baby, including doing the laundry and keeping the nursery clean.

A good baby nurse will:

- allow Mommy to rest by day and sleep by night
- start to teach the baby the difference between morning and night
- build Mommy's confidence
- show Mommy how to bathe the baby safely

- relay comforting stories about the other 271 babies she remembers screaming all night
- offer valuable tips based upon her experience
- allow Mommy and Daddy private time with the baby to continue bonding
- try not to get on Mommy's nerves

Your friends **are** the best source for a baby nurse. If they can steer you in the right direction, proceed, since this is a short-term relationship. If you are in a new city or if you are the first of your friends to have a baby, consult local nursing employment agencies. Ask the following questions before making the final decision:

☐ Does she smoke?

☐ Is she easy to have around? (This woman will live in your house.)

☐ Is she domineering and controlling (her way or no way) or does she present you with the different options and involve you in the decisions?

☐ Does she go about her business or does she follow you around all day and talk to you?

☐ Where does she sleep? (Most nurses prefer to sleep in the nursery.)

Mommy's Housekeeper

The term "housekeeper" is a catch-all phrase describing a woman who is hired to take care of the baby and clean the house. The responsibilities of each housekeeper are as varied as the mommies who employ them. You must establish priorities about the way you would like your household run and the type of person you're looking for to run it. The "Considerable Diddables" will bring to mind the needs all mommies should consider.

"Considerable Diddables"
Taking Care of Mommy's Priorities for the Perfect Housekeeper

Directions: Place a number (1-10) in the box beside each diddable in order of importance to you.

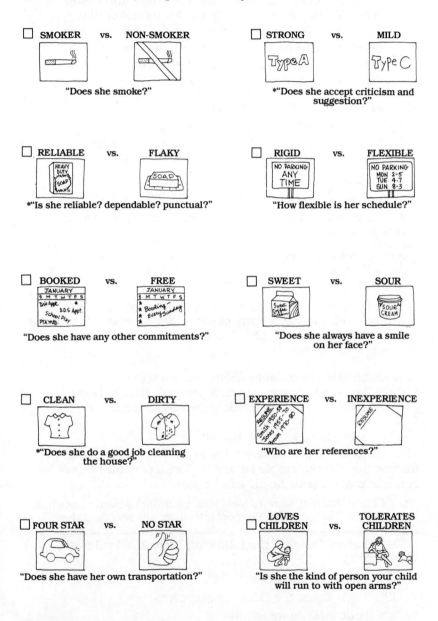

☐ SMOKER   vs.   NON-SMOKER

"Does she smoke?"

☐ STRONG   vs.   MILD

*"Does she accept criticism and suggestion?"

☐ RELIABLE   vs.   FLAKY

*"Is she reliable? dependable? punctual?"

☐ RIGID   vs.   FLEXIBLE

"How flexible is her schedule?"

☐ BOOKED   vs.   FREE

"Does she have any other commitments?"

☐ SWEET   vs.   SOUR

"Does she always have a smile on her face?"

☐ CLEAN   vs.   DIRTY

*"Does she do a good job cleaning the house?"

☐ EXPERIENCE   vs.   INEXPERIENCE

"Who are her references?"

☐ FOUR STAR   vs.   NO STAR

"Does she have her own transportation?"

☐ LOVES CHILDREN   vs.   TOLERATES CHILDREN

"Is she the kind of person your child will run to with open arms?"

*Questions to ask references.

Designing the perfect "Help Wanted" ad

Mommy doesn't need to have a creative writing degree to prepare a straight forward, informative, "Help Wanted" ad. Here are two suggested formats:

> Mature housekeeper wanted for busy household. Must love children, be flexible with days and hours. Seeking long term relationship. Non-smoker and references, please. 14 Mile area. 299-4576

> Reliable housekeeper wanted for adorable five month old. Three days a week. Light housekeeping. Own car. Telegraph area. 624-4094

Be sure to include the following:

- Type of position
- Type of household (working mother, busy household)
- Type of work (light housekeeping vs. heavy cleaning)
- Number of days per week (hours, if necessary)
- Location, including main cross streets or community areas
- Phone number (hours available if necessary)
- "References, please"

Generally, the best days to run a "Help Wanted" ad are on Sunday and Thursday. (Many papers offer a weekend combination rate; we advise you skip it and advertise in the edition that suits you best.)

It is absolutely essential to check references! Your child's life is being placed in this person's hands. Don't be lazy just because you think someone sounds "nice"!

Hiring

The final step in this progression is the face-to-face interview. Review the "Considerable Diddables" with the interviewee to confirm that all your needs will be met.

(**TCOM Hint:** You may want to have your children present to see how they react to "her" and more importantly, how she reacts to them.)

TCOM Survey Results: the following household rules are "top priority":

1. 35% The Children Come First
2. 33% Don't Open the Door for Strangers
3. 32% Follow My Instructions

The Babysitter

A babysitter is someone who keeps your children safe and happy ("minds the store") while you are out of the house. As a general rule, sitters are responsible for the care of the child and cleaning up after themselves. They are not responsible for cleaning the home or doing errands.

A babysitter is usually paid by the hour, while a housekeeper is usually paid by the day. And while the term "sitter" commonly refers to a neighborhood teenager, it embraces everyone from Grandma to a babysitting agency.

Where to Find

- Ask neighbors and friends

- Call the local high school

- Check the telephone book for babysitting agencies (Beware: expensive. However, they do have women who specialize in newborn care when you have no other alternative.)

- Church groups, community organizations

Mommy's Ten Commandments for the Sitter

1. Thou shalt never leave a new sitter with any child, especially a baby, without an adjustment period. (Don't pull a "revolving door": she comes in, you swing out. Always say "goodbye" to your child and tell her when you will return.)

2. Thou shalt never leave the house without the sitter knowing where you will be and when you will return. (If you will be unavailable, have someone who is "on call".)

3. Thou shalt never assume the sitter can do things the way you want them done. (Teach her to diaper, wash, and dress the baby in accordance with your standards.)

4. Thou shalt never hire a sitter without first checking out her references or speaking to her family.

5. Thou shalt never have your sitter treat or take care of a sick child without your explicit written instructions.

6. Thou shalt never allow your child to be taken from the premises without your full knowledge and permission!

7. Thou shalt never forget to explain all emergency and safety precautions, including burglar alarm system, double

locks, fuses, flashlights, thermostats and emergency call list (doctor, police, fire, etc.).

8. Thou shalt never leave the house without the sitter knowing the complete bedtime routine: rituals, favorite books and animals, pacifiers, "blankie", and sleepers.

9. Thou shalt never make the sitter scrounge for Pepsi and chips. (Show her where the basics are located.)

10. Thou shalt never leave the house without reviewing Mommy's "Ten Commandments for the Sitter."

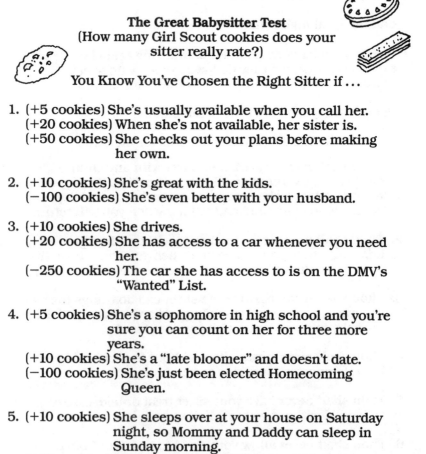

The Great Babysitter Test
(How many Girl Scout cookies does your sitter really rate?)

You Know You've Chosen the Right Sitter if ...

1. (+5 cookies) She's usually available when you call her.
   (+20 cookies) When she's not available, her sister is.
   (+50 cookies) She checks out your plans before making her own.

2. (+10 cookies) She's great with the kids.
   (−100 cookies) She's even better with your husband.

3. (+10 cookies) She drives.
   (+20 cookies) She has access to a car whenever you need her.
   (−250 cookies) The car she has access to is on the DMV's "Wanted" List.

4. (+5 cookies) She's a sophomore in high school and you're sure you can count on her for three more years.
   (+10 cookies) She's a "late bloomer" and doesn't date.
   (−100 cookies) She's just been elected Homecoming Queen.

5. (+10 cookies) She sleeps over at your house on Saturday night, so Mommy and Daddy can sleep in Sunday morning.
   (+15 cookies) She whips up a batch of fresh blueberry pancakes ... the kids' favorite.
   (+25 cookies) She keeps another batch on warm until you awaken.

6. (+10 cookies) Her rates are fair and competitive.
   (+5 cookies) Higher wages don't begin until midnight.
   (−125 cookies) She turns into a "pumpkin" at midnight.

7. (+10 cookies) She has a bright mind and excellent common
   sense.
   (+25 cookies) She's teaching your three year old Spanish.
   (−50 cookies) The phrase she's teaching is "donde esta
   the chocolates".

8. (+10 cookies) She stops on her way to pick up a large
   pizza with pepperoni and cheese for herself
   and the kids.
   (+20 cookies) She freezes the leftovers and cleans up the
   entire kitchen afterwards.
   (+150 cookies) She does the laundry, sweeps the floors,
   and paints the guest bedroom, too.

9. (+50 cookies) She responds quickly and maturely to your
   smoke detector alarm.
   (+250 cookies) She grabs the baby, runs to the neighbor's
   and calls the fire department.
   (−200 cookies) Four young, good-looking firemen are keeping her company when you return home.

10. (+15 cookies) She keeps the telephone line clear so you
    can always get through.
    (−100 cookies) She's on the phone half of the night.
    (+100 cookies) That means your mother-in-law couldn't
    get through.

200–800 cookies:
You win a merit badge! You've found a great babysitter. Code
her phone number in your telephone book and don't lend her
to your sister-in-law (or even your best friend).

(TCOM Hint: While we're on the subject, it's a universal "no-no"
to steal anybody's housekeeper, babysitter.)

5 cookies and below:
You goofed! By now you're well aware of your mistakes, since
she's probably made off with the four firemen, the policeman
from the DMV, or the captain of the football team! Have a glass
of milk with your cookies (if you have any left) and reread
this section.

Mommy's Childcare Alternatives

1. **Day-Care Centers and Family-Care Centers**

2. **Babysitting Co-ops** This is a good solution for a Mommy who needs free, experienced childcare for limited periods of time. Mommy watches another child in her home in exchange for an I.O.U. good for an equal number of hours of childcare for Mommy's child. (A good record-keeping system is essential to a successful babysitting co-op.)

   Advantages: It's free! You and your child get to meet neighborhood parents with whom you can share experiences and information. It's also a good source of playmates for your child.

   Disadvantages: Lack of consistency; your child doesn't have the same sitter all of the time. Also, you may get a tough child or a tough parent. (Consult the bibliography at the end of this book for rules and regulations on setting up your own babysitting co-op.)

3. **Grandmothers**

4. **The Mother's Helper** This helper is a step above a babysitter and a step below a housekeeper in terms of responsibility and wages. While most mother's helpers can be left alone with the children, she usually works along with Mommy to provide an extra pair of hands in household tasks (and daily outings).

EMS - 911
Fire - 555-1234
Police 555 2345

Help!

There's nothing funny about emergencies or making sure you're prepared for them. If you haven't already taken a first aid course, now is the time to do so. (Check with the YMCA, the American Red Cross, or your local community center.)

There are basic first aid instructions that all responsible mothers need to know: 1) Heimlich maneuver (choking), 2) How to handle ingested poisons, and 3) Artificial Respiration. If you don't take the time to learn any other type of first aid, **learn how to do these three!** Also, keep a good baby and child care handbook within reach.

(**TCOM Hint: Baby and Child Care,** Dr. Benjamin Spock. With over 30,000,000 copies sold, we think it's still the best!)

Emergency Instructions

Before you hire your first sitter or housekeeper, you must sit down and make up a list of all pertinent phone numbers and place this list in clear sight near the phone. Include these phone numbers: EMS (Emergency Medical Service), Fire, Police, Poison Control, Pediatrician, relative and/or neighbor, close friend (second in command if you can't be reached).

Ready Alert
(Other essentials)

Childproofing: The first time you put your child down in one spot, and she proudly moves herself to another is the precise moment you should childproof your home. Make a clean sweep of your home at the child's level, removing everything that could harm her or that she could break. Once again, consult your baby care manual for tips on accomplishing this successfully and safely.

(**TCOM Hint:** Don't forget to install childproof safety locks on all cabinets containing cleaning supplies and other toxic substances.)

Smoke detectors: This is a must, along with flame retardant clothing, bedding, fire extinguishers, and baby decals. (Baby decals, also called "Tot Finders", are stickers placed on windows that alert firemen to the presence of a child in that room. Consult your local fire department for use and availability.)

Burglar alarms: This provides Mommy, as well as the entire family, with a total sense of protection. While a good security alarm system can be extremely costly, it's hard to put a price on your family's well-being and Mommy's peace of mind.

Before reaching the hospital Annie
Was as modest and shy as a granny,
This was quickly removed
Since delivery behooved
That she boldly exhibit her fanny!

Inside Out

The Miracle of Labor, Delivery and Recovery

"Betty went through it and said it was ..."

"Louise went through it and said it wasn't ..."

"Even Diane went through it three times (Why would she keep doing it if it was so ...)"

There is no other time in Mommy's life during which she spends so many hours for so many months arranging, agonizing and anticipating. "Who will examine me? What if I scream? What if I pass out? What if I pass gas (or worse)? What if I need a C-section? Will the baby be okay ..."

These fears are as common to pregnancy as heartburn and the middle of the night "tinkle".

"Inside Out" will take Mommy through everything that might happen, from the first contraction to the first, "Congratulations!" First-time Mommies will get the real "scoop" on who will stick what, where, when and why. Second-time Mommies will be reminded of how terrific they were the first time around and how quickly they've forgotten it all.

Read on. And, the next time you talk to Betty, Louise, and Diane, give them "our best."

The Beginning Signs of Labor

Call your doctor if . . .

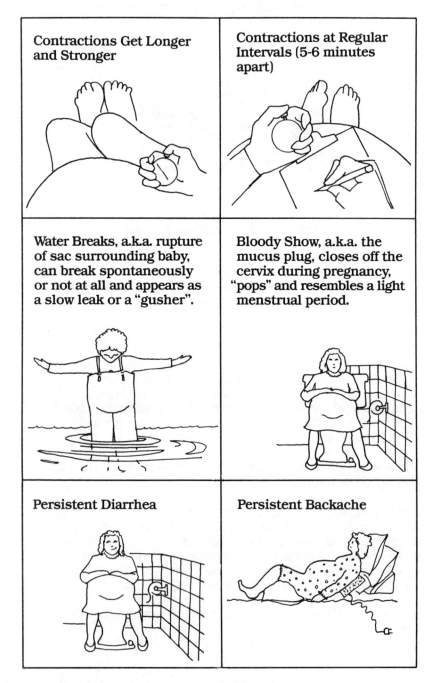

Contractions Get Longer and Stronger

Contractions at Regular Intervals (5-6 minutes apart)

Water Breaks, a.k.a. rupture of sac surrounding baby, can break spontaneously or not at all and appears as a slow leak or a "gusher".

Bloody Show, a.k.a. the mucus plug, closes off the cervix during pregnancy, "pops" and resembles a light menstrual period.

Persistent Diarrhea

Persistent Backache

- Your contractions are so close that by the time one ends, the next one is half over

- You see your baby smiling back at you

- Your water broke . . . last Thursday

- Your doctor calls **you** wondering where you are

- Your "nesting instinct" peaked . . . you've not only recleaned your entire house, but you've worked your way down the block

(Once you think you're in labor, do not eat!) And, if you stop on the way to the hospital, don't buy two "extra-crispy" dinners, unless Daddy is famished or your best friend is along for the ride.

Most hospitals and doctors do not allow Mommy to eat during labor because:

- If you should need general anesthesia and if you should vomit, you may aspirate the contents of your full stomach into your lungs

- Diarrhea could occur in early labor (digestion usually stops)

If you are starving, ask your doctor—you may be able to have tea and clear broths.

The Hospital Procedure

Your suspicions are confirmed. Your doctor and the baby are on the way!

1. **Off to the hospital.** (Mommy may or may not be driving, depending on Daddy's condition.)

    - Get there safely. (Don't run the red light of the busiest intersection in town.)

    - Get there quickly. (Take a dry run in advance to master the most direct route.)

    - Get there in time. (It's really not exciting to deliver the baby in the back seat of a Cougar.)

2. **At Emergency.** Daddy will turn Mommy over to the medical staff at the Emergency entrance.

   (**TCOM Hint:** There is no need for Daddy to announce Mommy's arrival, since as soon as she is spotted, the wheels will be set in motion.)

3. **Up to Maternity.** Mommy will be escorted to the maternity floor by a nurse or orderly.

   Upon arrival, Mommy will be asked the following questions, provided she isn't busy "pushing":
   - name, age, due date, doctor's name?
   - have pre-admission forms been submitted?
   - first baby, second baby?
   - any complications or medical problems that should be known immediately?
   - when food was last eaten?

4. **On to the table.** Mommy will put on a hospital gown and be examined vaginally by the intern or chief resident to determine the extent of dilation and effacement. (It is unlikely that Mommy's own obstetrician will be present.) At this time she will also be asked:
   - duration and frequency of contractions?
   - bag of waters broken?
   - bloody show?

5. **Into the labor room.** Mommy will be admitted and her doctor will be notified.

   (**TCOM Hint:** Don't "pump up" for the "big event" ahead of schedule, only to be deflated. It's disappointing and depressing. Don't rush to the hospital at the first twinge. **Call the doctor and follow his advice.** It's extremely unlikely that a baby, especially a first-time baby, will be born within an hour or two. Wait for significant signals from your body or your doctor!)

According to a study of 10,000 deliveries at Johns Hopkins Hospital in Baltimore, the most frequently reported total length of labor was seven hours for primiparas (first babies) and four hours for multiparas (second or more babies).

Mommy's Rights as an Obstetric Patient

**(Guide to Mommy's rights as she progresses
through the various stages of labor.)**

1 cm Mommy has the right to wake up
her husband.

2 cm Mommy has the right to be considered
for admittance.

3 cm Mommy has the right to rest between
contractions.

4 cm Mommy has the right to be coached.

5 cm Mommy has the right to be spurred on, comforted
and encouraged.

6 cm Mommy has the right to request pain medication
(or that the intern move out of the way of her
focal point!)

7 cm Mommy has the right to nausea, chills, cramps,
and shaking.

8 cm Mommy has the right to lose her modesty, her
dignity, and last night's dinner.

9 cm Mommy has the right to call her husband every
name in the book.

10 cm Mommy has the right to push.

Questioning the Old Standbys

Prepping (partial or complete shave): thought to
prevent infection, but no longer proven.

Routine I.V.'s: thought to keep veins open in case
of emergency. However, a pregnant woman's veins are
easy to find quickly if there is an emergency.

Episiotomy: thought to be for Mommy's safety, however no longer proven.

Fetal monitors: machines that force Mommy to remain
on back or side. Nurse could monitor Mommy without
restrictions.

Silver nitrate in baby's eyes, required by law: why
should the baby be subjected to this if the Mommy
is gonorrhea free?

Meet the Hospital Staff

Staff Member	Coat Length	Education
Medical Student	Short blazer	Third year medical school
Intern (First year resident)	Between hip and knee	Graduated from medical school last June; this is the next educational step
Chief Resident (Fourth year resident)	At the knee	Graduated from medical school; has completed three years of residency
Obstetrician (OB) 	Below the knee	Graduated from medical school, has completed residency (fellowship optional)
Student Nurse	Scrub dress with name badge bearing school name	In nursing school
O.B. Nurse	Scrub dress	Graduate Registered Nurse (R.N.)

Training	What he/she should be doing for you!	What he/she should NOT be doing to you!
Seeing first delivery	Take history; make small talk; get in way	Attempt to get complete history while you're in active labor. ("Did you ever get your tonsils out? What hospital? Did it hurt? What flavor ice cream did you prefer...")
Residencies start in July, therefore he'll be more experienced in in the spring	Vaginal exam upon admittance; assist in delivery	Give you your fifth vaginal exam in one hour. (If he's looking for something to do, refer him to the Mommy in Bed #4.)
Three years of doing deliveries and everything else	Emergency delivery; emergency C-section; assist in regular delivery or C-section	Begin a C-section before the anesthesiologist shows up!
Years of experience	Deliver your beautiful baby	Predict the sex of the baby before it is born. (It doesn't matter how good his batting average is, he's got to be wrong some of the time. Ever hear of Murphy's Law?)
Seeing first delivery	Vital signs, ice chips; help make you comfortable	Bring you a full dinner tray
Experienced in labor and delivery nursing	Prep; help coach watch monitor; perform standard nursing duties	Critique your "performance" while you're in labor

65

The Labor Room

Description: hospital bed; nightstand with monitor on top or on separate table; bathroom with sink and toilet.

Facilities/supplies: examining gloves (for vaginal examination); Amni hooks (to break water; looks like long crocheting needle); emesis basin (for vomiting); bed pans (for urinating or bowel movements); catheters (for "shut downs"); I.V. poles (to hold I.V.'s); chairs (to hold Daddy).

In attendance: Mommy, Daddy, labor nurse, student nurse; occasional visits by intern, chief resident and/or OB.

What's happening (general procedures):

- Mommy's vital signs will be monitored: temperature, pulse and blood pressure.

- Mommy may be prepped, including a shave/mini-shave of pubic hair and/or enema.

   (**TCOM Hint:** Find out your doctor's or hospital's policy in advance, so you will be psychologically prepped, as well.)

- Mommy may be monitored electronically by the following:

   External monitor: two belts attached to Mommy's waist:
   1. above the pubic hair line: measures frequency of baby's heartbeat
   2. below navel: measures Mommy's uterine contractions

   Internal monitor: plastic tube with wires, attached to electrodes; inserted into Mommy's vagina and attached to baby's scalp. (The electrodes do a more accurate job of monitoring the baby's heartbeat and can immediately alert the doctor to early warning signs of fetal distress.)

- Daddy will return to Mommy's side after he's parked the car, filled out the necessary admission forms and officially admitted Mommy.

- Mommy and Daddy will work toward the goal: **100% effacement** (thinning of the cervix, measured in percentages, 0-100%); **dilation to 10 cm** (size of the round opening of the cervix, measured in centimeters).

Transition

The progression of labor between 8 and 10 centimeters is commonly referred to as "transition". This is both the shortest and the hardest part of labor.

Signs: extreme irritability; urge to push; rectal pressure; nausea; vomiting; cramps; shaking.

Just when you think you can't go on, your body and your doctor give you the "go ahead" and you can push as you contract to begin delivery.

The Delivery Room

Description: delivery table with stirrups; mirrors for Mommy to watch birth; long table with equipment; area for newborn [baby warmer, scale, oxygen, fluorescent light (heat)].

Facilities/supplies: forceps; metal basin for placenta; syringes; scissors for episiotomy; sutures for episiotomy; I.V.'s; blood pressure cuffs; bulb syringe to suction out baby's nose; clamp for umbilical cord; sterile drapes; lots and lots of gauze for blotting.

In attendance:
1. Mommy
2. Daddy
3. OB
4. Chief Resident
5. OB Nurse
6. Intern
7. Circulating Nurse
8. Med Student
9. Student Nurse
10. Anesthesiologist
11. Pediatrician
12. Pediatric Nurse

What's happening (general procedures): Mommy's legs are placed in stirrups; Mommy is draped with sterile cloth and prepped (washed with antiseptic); anesthesia is administered if necessary or requested (see "Mommy's Pain Medication Options"); episiotomy may be performed (small cut between vagina and anus to enlarge the birth ring and prevent it from painful tearing).

A few grunts and groans ... a few more pushes and pants ... and one big miracle!

Mommy's Pain Medication Options

Type	Common Name	*How Administered	How It Works
Psychological Pain Relief by Conditioned Reflex	Lamaze, Natural Childbirth	Coach	Control pain by breathing techniques focal point
Drugs			
Tranquilizers Often Given Together	Phenergan, Valium, Vistaril, Sparine	Resident or O.B.	Injection or I.V.
Analgesics	Demerol (long acting); Sublimaze (short acting)	Resident or O.B.	Injection or I.V.
Anesthesia			
General	Putting Mommy Out	Anesthesiologist or Nurse Anesthetist	Gas and I.V.
Regional	A. Spinal Many Mommies do not understand that a Spinal and a Saddle Block are the same. In both cases, the medication is injected in the same area. The only altering factor is the position of Mommy's body during the injection procedure.	Anesthesiologist	One injection into spinal column; Mommy *lays flat* to permit medicine to "rise", anesthesizing larger area.

Effects	Side Effects	TCOM Note:
Can work miracles	Blurred vision from staring at favorite "pin up" poster	Take this course whether or not you plan to use it; the breathing techniques and educational infor-
Relaxes Mommy; may control nausea and vomiting	May cause Mommy to sleep between contrac- tions making Lamaze training ineffective	mation are helpful. labor and can cross the placenta, enter- ing the baby's circu- lation; generally, "less is better!"
Diminishes sense of pain; increases pain threshold	May induce sleep	
Loss of con- sciousness (Ba-bye!)	Grogginess; disorientation	General anesthesia is rarely used except for emergency C-sections.

Numbs Mommy from below breast to toes (generally used for C-section); may last ½ hour to 2 hours depending on dosage.	May decrease Mommy's blood pressure; may develop head- aches; Mommy unable to push— usually use forceps.	

About Spinal side effects: The incidence of neurological problems following spinals is exceedingly rare—probably less than 1 in 10,000. (If back "problems" do occur they may be the result of lying on a hard table.) The incidence of headaches has decreased due to use of smaller needles. Lying flat after a Spinal does nothing to prevent a headache, but if a headache should occur, lying flat helps dramatically. Most headaches respond to hydra- tion and analgesics.

Type	Common Name	*How Administered	How It Works
	Saddleblock	Anesthesiologist	One injection into spinal column; Mommy must remain "seated" to permit medicine to "sink".
	B. Epidural (A caudal block has fallen out of favor because it requires more medication than an epidural and has a slightly higher chance of infection.)	Anesthesiologist	Catheter inserted in the space outside spinal column; medicine flows continuously; must be monitored constantly.
Local	Paracervical Block	Chief Resident or O.B.	Injection into perineum

Source:

James M. Feld, M.D.: Assistant Clinical Professor of Anesthesiology, Pritzker School of Medicine, University of Chicago; Associate Director of Intensive Care Unit, Michael Reese Hospital.

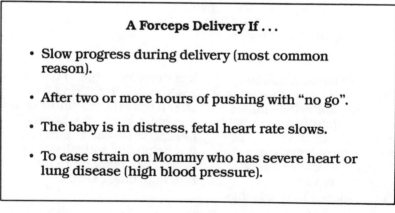

A Forceps Delivery If . . .

- Slow progress during delivery (most common reason).

- After two or more hours of pushing with "no go".

- The baby is in distress, fetal heart rate slows.

- To ease strain on Mommy who has severe heart or lung disease (high blood pressure).

Effects	Side Effects	TCOM Note:
Numbs Mommy in area where she sits	Same as Spinal 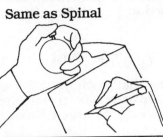	
Numbs Mommy from belly button to toes; can "dial down" when it's time to push so Mommy will have urge, or use forceps.	May slow first stage of labor progress, but rarely longer than 30 minutes, can decrease Mommy's blood pressure.	Commonly referred to as "The Champagne of Anesthesia". However, since an epidural can run for hours, an anesthesiologist must be present throughout. Not all hospitals provide this option.
Numbs area between anus and vagina for episiotomy; doesn't interfere in pushing		

A C-Section if . . .

- The baby is in distress.

- Mommy is in **real** distress.

- Labor is not progressing because the baby is too large for pelvis.

- Baby is in unusual position.

- Cervix will not dilate.

- Baby's head will not engage in birth canal.

- Placenta separates prematurely.

- Placenta Previa (placenta first) blocks the baby.

(5-20% of first-time Mommies end up having a C-Section. Most first-time C-Sections are not planned in advance, they are decided during labor.)

The afterbirth: (You can put the cameras away now, Daddies!) If you are under an anesthetic, you won't even be aware of this. However, if you have "gone natural", you will feel one more giant contraction to expel the afterbirth (the placenta and membrane).

Bonding

The special moment that Mommy, Daddy, and baby share immediately after the baby is born is referred to as the "bonding" period. This may last anywhere from one minute to one hour.

TCOM Survey Results: 73% of the Mommies bonded with Daddy and baby. The average length of time for bonding was 20 minutes.

Here are the most common types of bonding:

Crazy Glue Bond: The baby never leaves Mommy's side until he's 18.

Rubber Cement Bond: Cementing of love and security between Mommy, Daddy, and baby; Daddy bonds with baby (good feelings rub off), Mommy bonds with baby (good feelings rub off).

Elmer's Bond: All purpose; Mommy, Elmer and baby bond for 10-15 minutes.

School Paste Bond: Your four year old joins in bonding by attaching herself to Mommy, Daddy, and baby with the help of construction paper, blunt edge scissors, and wooden sticks.

Clear Glue Bond: Mommy takes a dab at bonding, but becomes unglued from the exhaustion of delivery.

Filming the Big Event

You will want to make a decision well in advance regarding photography, since the birth of your child is a "one take" production.

Whether you use Daddy's Polaroid, your brother-in-law's Instamatic, or your Uncle Harry's Bell & Howell sound movie camera, don't miss the opporturnity to preserve this euphoric moment.

(**TCOM Hint:** Instant cameras give you the opportunity to snap away and have immediate pictures that Daddy can take home and gaze at all night long!)

The Recovery Room

Description: 4–8 hospital beds in large room separated by curtains; desk; phone; supply cabinet.

Facilities/supplies: blood pressure cuffs; thermometers; I.V. poles; catheters; blankets; water basin; towels; soap; pads and belts; food and/or drink; phone to call best friend!

In attendance: Mommy #1, Mommy #2, Mommy #3, Mommy #4 ... and recovery nurse(s).

What's happening (general procedures): vital signs: temperature, pressure, pulse; clean up: wash, pad and belt, ice for stitches and hemorrhoids; food (optional). Length of stay is approximately one hour or more, depending upon condition and drugs/anesthesia wearing off.

(**TCOM Hint:** Feel free to ask for glass of juice, cup of tea, etc.)

TCOM Survey Results:*

"How did you think you were going to feel **emotionally** during labor, delivery and recovery?"

1. scared/nervous   48%
2. excited   36%
3. happy   25%
4. in control   19%

"How did you really feel?"

1. happy   57%
2. scared/nervous   34%
3. emotionally drained   24%
4. out of control   16%

*Due to multiple responses, results do not total 100%.

TCOM Survey Results*:

"How did you think you were going to feel **physically** during labor, delivery and recovery?"

1. pain   86%
2. exhausted   28%
3. fine   19%

"How did you really feel?"

1. pain   74%
2. exhausted   24%
3. Less painful than anticipated   16%

*Due to multiple responses, results do not total 100%.

The Birthing Room

Description: bed (standard, queen, king); chairs, paintings, curtains, television, stereo (optional); attempt to simulate warm "home" environment.

Facilities/supplies: private room that can be turned into a delivery room. If all goes well, Mommy has the option to stay in the birthing room to deliver the baby "in bed". However, forceps, anesthesia or a C-Section delivery cannot be performed here.

In attendance: Mommy, Daddy, labor nurse, intern or chief resident, OB; (optional) Grandma, Grandpa, siblings, Aunt Gertie, Uncle Seymour (no pets, please).

What's happening: natural childbirth; no anesthesia is available, except a "local" for the episiotomy; only for low risk deliveries and Mommies who do not wish to have any drugs; I.V. 's are not routine and are usually only used in stress; continuous electronic monitoring is available, but not mandatory.

The Birthing Center

Latest trend; a series of birthing rooms in a center; Mommy usually stays 24 hours and returns home with baby; this is as close as you can get to an "at home" delivery with the protection of being close to a medical facility if necessary.

Don't wait until you pull up to the Emergency entrance to find out that the birthing room you've been counting on won't be completed until next spring. Draft a plan and discuss it with your obstetrician well in advance of your due date.

Once the decisions are out of the way, you can concentrate all of your efforts on the impending miracle.

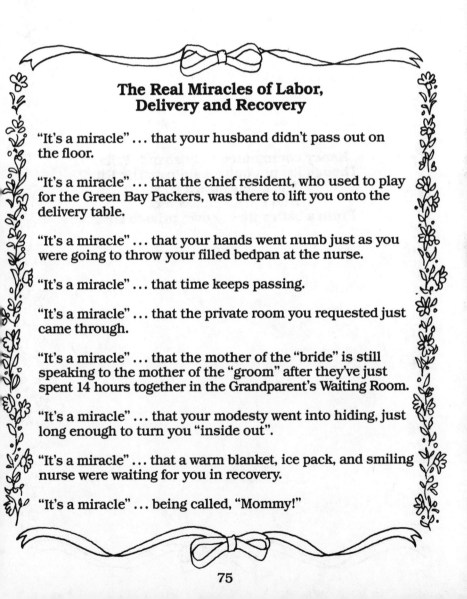

The Real Miracles of Labor, Delivery and Recovery

"It's a miracle" ... that your husband didn't pass out on the floor.

"It's a miracle" ... that the chief resident, who used to play for the Green Bay Packers, was there to lift you onto the delivery table.

"It's a miracle" ... that your hands went numb just as you were going to throw your filled bedpan at the nurse.

"It's a miracle" ... that time keeps passing.

"It's a miracle" ... that the private room you requested just came through.

"It's a miracle" ... that the mother of the "bride" is still speaking to the mother of the "groom" after they've just spent 14 hours together in the Grandparent's Waiting Room.

"It's a miracle" ... that your modesty went into hiding, just long enough to turn you "inside out".

"It's a miracle" ... that a warm blanket, ice pack, and smiling nurse were waiting for you in recovery.

"It's a miracle" ... being called, "Mommy!"

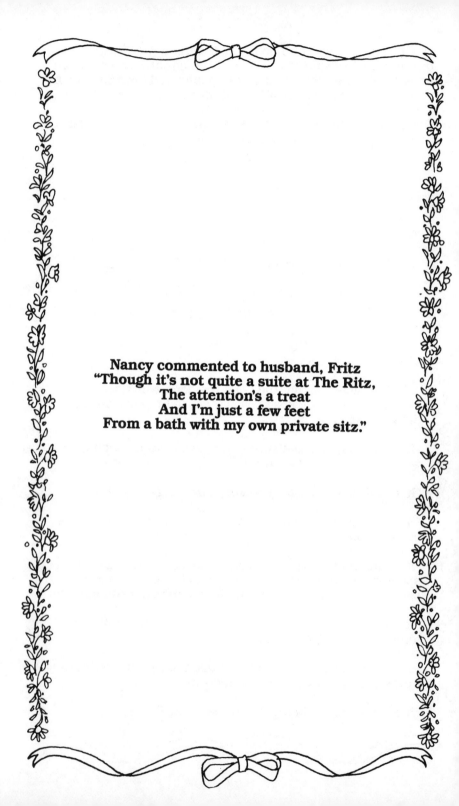

Nancy commented to husband, Fritz
"Though it's not quite a suite at The Ritz,
The attention's a treat
And I'm just a few feet
From a bath with my own private sitz."

The Hospitality Suite

Nursing Mommy Back to Health

"Welcome to the hospitality suite. If this is your first stay with us, let me take a moment to familiarize you with the accommodations. If you've been with us before, perhaps you'd like to note some of the changes ..."

Private Room with Bath

Description: one room with one single bed, one television, one phone; private bath with toilet and sink, shower (optional); regular or deluxe varieties.

Advantages: private; can rest when you desire; great for spending many happy, quiet moments with baby and husband; can turn off television and phone for naps; plenty of room for flowers; plenty of peace and quiet (if such a thing is possible in the hospital).

Disadvantages: loneliness; no one to help you attack the gorgeous fruit basket at 2 a.m.; no one to admire your beautiful flowers; no one to share toilet facilities with; no one to sit with and drool over the latest soap opera "flame"; popular hide-out for nurses ... on or off break.

Cost: additional cost, ranging from $5-50 per day above a semi-private.

How Mommy Can Get a Private
(without getting court-martialed)

Private rooms are usually in demand, since the supply is limited. While some hospitals offer "privates" on a first come/ first served basis, many test Mommy's creative ingenuity. Here are a few suggestions:

1. Marry the hospital director.

2. Picket the nurses station ... nude. (Guaranteed to get you a private ... in the psycho ward!)

3. Ask Uncle Charlie to donate a hospital wing.

4. Bribe the admissions lady, who assigns rooms. (She loves nightgowns and coupon books.)

5. Be so obnoxious no one could stand to have you as a roommate.

6. Be a pest — keep asking your doctor, nurse, nurse's aid and clergy.

7. Get down on your knees and beg.

Semi-Private with Bath

Description: one room with two single beds, one or two televisions; one or two phones with one or two lines; private bath with toilet and sink; one window. (Usually inhabited by two Mommies, one of whom is definitely in control. See "Art of Being a Good Roommate".)

Advantages: 24 hour companionship; someone with whom to share stories, visitors and phone conversations; able to enjoy each other's flowers, candy and "soaps".

Disadvantages: not for the modest Mommy who likes privacy, peace and old "B" movies; start doing your "kegels" immediately, since you'll need strong bladder control to wait your turn; incompatible Mommies.

Cost: included in many health insurance policies; if your plan excludes this option, consider upgrading yourself to a semi-private from a ward for approximately $5-10 per day.

The Art of Being a Good Roommate
Bed One vs. Bed Two

The Ward

Description: one room with four single beds, two televisions, two to four phones with one to four lines; bathroom and sink are down the hall. Usually inhabited by four women: three are playing poker, eating bologna sandwiches, and watching "Johnny Carson" – the fourth is screaming for the Admission's nurse!

Advantages: nonstop companionship; three more labor and delivery stories; three more chances to swap your Apple Betty for a piece of chocolate cake; three more husband's to meet; three more babies to bond with. (Great for Mommies with voyeur tendencies!)

Disadvantages: wards are like mini-bowling banquets – people love to socialize, share, talk, eat and most of all, never sleep. If you are looking for some "R & R", you're in the wrong place! (A minor disadvantage is restricted visitations because of the numbers and the need for "crowd control".)

Cost: if you have health insurance, you are covered for this accommodation.

(**TCOM Hint:** We recommend you find a hospital that provides semi-private care to get sufficient rest, medical attention, and bonding time with husband and baby.)

Rooming-In

This term means just that – it's Mommy and baby from start to finish. Mommy cares for baby completely (nursing staff will supervise when requested and will answer questions), and the baby remains in the room with Mommy for the duration of the hospital stay. (The only time the baby is gone is for routine tests.)

Advantages: Mommy learns to care for the baby right away (excellent if Mommy won't have any help once she gets home).

Disadvantages: doesn't give Mommy time to rest and recuperate from trauma of birth.

(**TCOM Hint:** Give this option serious thought. You'll have this "little bundle of joy" for the rest of your life. Don't feel guilty about getting some long overdue rest now to give yourself a good headstart when you get home. Consider a compromise. Check with the nursing staff/nursery to see if you can have the baby during the day and return him to the nursery at night.)

Little Known Facts
(What the Hospital will do for You)

Once the baby is born and you are settled into your own room, the fun begins (not for you, but for the nursing staff!). The first 24 hours are the worst, since Mommy must be checked every four hours or less, for "postpartum vital signs": blood pressure, pulse, temperature, and tummy squeeze (the nurse pushes on your uterus to make sure it's snapping back into shape.) Yes! You will be awakened—hope you're the type of Mommy who can fall back to sleep easily!

After the first day you will be checked three times daily (once each shift) for "vital signs", hemorrhoids, and stitches. You will **constantly** be asked how often you have urinated and, the infamous, "Have you moved your bowels yet?" ("Yes, I've moved them to Cincinnati . . . would you like the forwarding address?")

In addition, here are some "little known facts" about what the hospital will do for you:

Nurses: They will provide you (upon request) with ice packs for stitches, hemorrhoids, and swollen breasts. If you are breast feeding, they will give you mammal nipple cream, pads, nipple shields, and a rubber breast pump. If you are not breast feeding, ask to be bound immediately!

(**TCOM Hint:** Do not wait until your milk comes in or you will be hot, sore, swollen and in PAIN! In addition, your doctor may prescribe "dry up" pills which may or may not work. Thus, it's a good precautionary measure to be bound.)

The nurses will also turn their heads when Daddy or Grandma brings Mommy a treat, from corned beef on rye to her favorite lasagna.

(**TCOM Hint:** Begin getting your body in shape now. Let Daddy bring fresh fruit in season for those hungry cravings and pass up the Big Mac, large fries, and shake.)

The nurses will also provide Mommy with the necessary paperwork for birth certificates. These must be filled out and signed before Mommy leaves the hospital. Don't forget, or William James Houston III will be John Doe, No. 4,862 forever!

Housekeeping: The housekeeping staff will keep your room clean and change your bed daily. In addition, they will stock your supplies, provide you with (upon request) extra pillows, blankets, towels, and nighties and constantly replenish your fresh ice water.

Dietary: The dietary department will provide "scrumptious" meals of your choosing. Extra dietary trays may be purchased every noon and evening for Daddy. (Do let the dietary office know in advance—the cost is approximately $4-7 per meal.) This is a nice treat for both Daddy and Mommy!

Many hospitals also provide a complimentary congratulatory dinner for new Mommies and Daddies, complete with a bottle of wine. (In many hospitals, the pharmacist also doubles as the sommelier.) This is a nice, romantic touch.

Operator: Many Mommies don't know they can have their phone shut off during naptime or special quiet moments with the baby! Upon request, the operator will hold Mommy's calls morning, noon, or night.

Photographer: The nursery photographer will try to capture the essence of your newborn's beauty. Unfortunately, he'll probably miss, but we have yet to meet a new Mommy who can resist buying the hospital's "portrait plan".

(TCOM Hint: Have Daddy bring his own camera and snap away. This is a cheaper and wiser option, since this will provide you with different poses and faces of your baby over the four or five days.)

The nursery: The nursery nurses are wonderful! If asked, they will show you everything from how to diaper to how to feed the baby. Don't overlook this valuable resource. If you have any anxieties or questions, ask!

Nursery visitation policies differ across the country. Generally, the baby is brought to Mommy at feeding time and stays with Mommy for one hour. The most popular scheduling is "6-10-2" due to the nursing staff shift scheduling of "7-11-3". Bottle feeding Mommies: The nursery will keep your baby during the 2 A.M. feeding and at other feedings, and also upon request. Don't feel guilty! If you need extra time to recuperate and rest, take advantage of this built-in help. Breast feeding Mommies: Upon request, the nursery may keep your baby for one feeding daily, in which they will give the baby water. Check with your doctor and hospital.

Often the nursery visitation rules lighten up on the weekends, due to reduced staffing. Thus, many hospitals permit Mommy to keep the baby much of the day Saturday and Sunday without formal "rooming-in". (If your hospital stay should include a weekend, and if you want to spend additional time with the baby, ask!)

How to Take a Community Shower

The maternity floor is like the locker room after the big game. While the coach and a few key players might be lucky enough to take a private shower, everyone else goes the "community route". Here are some tips for cleaning up Mommy's act.

Your first shower after childbirth is a unique experience. You won't believe how sore your bottom is, how big your stomach is, and how long it takes you!

Avoid the lines: Shower before the 6 a.m. feeding (5-5:30 a.m.) or after the 10 a.m. feeding (11 a.m.-Noon). The worst time is anywhere in between!

Organize yourself: there's nothing worse than having your "number called", only to find that you left your conditioner, razor blade, and clean pads back in the room.

Fill your water basin with all the things you'll need: soap, shampoo, conditioner, squirt bottle, fresh pad and belt, Tucks, hemorrhoid spray, disposable wash cloths, towels, one clean pair of underpants, one clean bra, one pair of disposable footies.

Once you're "in", here's the plan: **Breasts:** wash in gentle circular motion with a clean cloth to prevent infection (don't let the hot water run directly on your chest, since it stimulates your breasts and induces milk flow). **Vaginal area:** wash in a downward stroke from front to back; use the squirt bottle to rinse perineum (if squirt bottle is unavailable, cup hands and splash water gently). You can take it from here, as long as the hot water lasts!

After you've dried off, hook on your pad with Tucks **immediately,** then put on your clean underwear, bra, robe, and slippers and head back to the room! (Please don't forget to clean up the shower for the next Mommy!)

(**TCOM Hint:** Finish dressing in your room, since it's cooler and it allows another Mommy to use the shower. Puff, powder, and primp at your leisure.)

When to "lie" to the Nurse!

Please don't misunderstand. We're not advocating lying. However, it has been brought to our attention from the survey results that the majority of Mommies did "fib" occasionally to the nurse.

Now, we could have disregarded this part of the survey. But, feeling obliged to impart the entire results, we thought it our duty to pass them on to you and, let your conscience be your guide!

- Not receiving your dinner tray
  (lying vs. I'll start my diet tomorrow)

- Passing off your friend as your sister for visitation
  (lying vs. loneliness)

- Number of sitz baths taken
  (lying vs. lecture)

- Telling the doctor how wonderful you feel
  (lying vs. another day in the hospital)

Gifts of Appreciation

Everyone likes to be appreciated and the nursing staff is no exception. If you've had a cooperative, helpful bunch, tell them.

(**TCOM Hint:** Upon your departure consider donating one of your floral arrangements or a big box of candy for all of the nurses to share!)

In their quest to extend their good wishes
Friends and neighbors were most expeditious,
On the fragile excuse
That they might be of use
They dropped in at times most inauspicious.

Homecoming

The First Week
(Hooray for the HOME Team!)

It's a beautiful morning. The birds are chirping, the sun is shining—the day you've been anxiously awaiting is here. You feel great, having just knocked off the Dietary Department "special": a crisp rasher of bacon, perfectly prepared sunny-side-up eggs, and a large glass of freshly-squeezed orange juice. If you weren't on top of the world before, you certainly are now ... the nurse just informed you that your "little angel" slept through the night at four days old. You take a long, hot, relaxing shower. As you look down at your body you see your old shape has returned. At 10 A.M. you're packed, dressed and ready for hospital discharge. Your husband arrives with a dozen, long-stem red roses and sweeps you, the baby, and the flowers away in his shiny new Marina Blue Chevy ...

If it's mind games you're looking for, have we got a game for you...The **TCOM** Great Homecoming Game

See what a typical first day at home can really be like. To play the game, just follow the squares from your hospital bed to your home bed. You'll be a winner if you can spot the 20 "no-no's" hidden within the game. Good luck!

The Great Homecoming Game

Rules:

Follow the squares from your hospital bed to your home bed. You'll be a winner (THE HOMECOMING QUEEN) if you can spot the 20 "no-no's" hidden on the board.

Time Out

| 6:30 YOU WATCH BABY SO NURSE CAN EAT HOT FOOD | 6:50 NURSE RELIEVES YOU | 7:00 SIT DOWN AT TABLE - FIND ONLY SOY SAUCE & RICE LEFT | 7:15 EVERYONE LEAVES... YOU WITH DIRTY DISHES | 7:20 GO TO BATHROOM | 7:30 FIND HUSBAND ASLEEP ON SOFA | 7:35 CLEAN-UP KITCHEN | 9:35 LEAVE KITCHEN |

Time Out

| 6:25 EVERYONE IS SEATED FOR DINNER | 6:20 WING HONG DELIVERS | 6:00 GO UPSTAIRS TO FRESHEN UP | 5:55 PHONE RINGS | 5:38 GO TO BATHROOM | 5:35 - DOORBELL- UPS MAN (GRATEFUL, HE CAN'T STAY FOR DINNER) |

Field Goal

| 2:48 ENTER KITCHEN GUESTS LOOK AT YOU WITH FORKS IN HAND + EMPTY PLATES | 2:53 DISH UP COFFEECAKE FOR (16) | 2:54 SIT DOWN TO JOIN THEM | 2:55 -PHONE RINGS- SISTER FROM DENVER | 3:15 GO UPSTAIRS TO UNPACK | 4:00 12 SUITCASES LATER- YOU DECIDE TO TAKE A NAP. | 4:08 AWAKENED BY HUNGER PAINS |

Time Out

| -DOORBELL- ENTER: UNCLE CHALIE + AUNT BETTY | 2:40 -EMERGE- IN SWEAT & GO DOWNSTAIRS | 2:00 GUESTS EAT YOU GO TO BATHROOM | 1:55 PEEK AT BABY | 1:50 PHONE RINGS | 1:45 WHIP UP MUSHROOM & SPINACH OMELETS FOR (14) | 1:36 - DOORBELL- ENTER: UNCLE FRED+ AUNT HELEN |

Incomplete Pass ——→|

| 11:24 MOMMY PASSES OUT FLOWERS | 11:26 MOMMY PASSES OUT! | 11:30 NURSE REVIVES MOMMY+ WHEELS MOMMY+ BABY TO CAR | 11:35 MOMMY PUTS BABY IN CAR SEAT | 11:37 DADDY PUTS BABY IN CAR SEAT | 11:45 MOMMY+DADDY PUT BABY IN CAR SEAT | 11:47 DADDY PUTS MOMMY IN BACK ON TOP OF TWO SUITCASES |

| 11:22 MOMMY PASSES OUT CANDY | | | | | | |
| 11:20 MOMMY PASSES OUT GIFTS | 11:15 NURSERY DISCHARGES BABY | 11:00 HUSBAND RETURNS TO ROOM- KISSES MOMMY+ BABY- GRABS SUITCASES + HEADS FOR CAR ♡ | 10:50 HUSBAND RETURNS TO ROOM- KISSES MOMMY + BABY- GRABS SUITCASES + HEADS FOR CAR ♡ | 10:40 HUSBAND RETURNS TO ROOM- KISSES MOMMY+ BABY- GRABS SUITCASES + HEADS FOR CAR ♡ | | |

Kick-Off   Time Out

HOSPITAL

| 5:30 GET UP | 5:35 GO TO BATHROOM | 6:00 FEED BABY | 6:45 TAKE SHOWER | 7:15 GET DRESSED | 7:30 EAT BREAKFAST | 7:50 PACK FIRST THREE BAGS |

88

Answers:

Overpacked 7:50-9:30, Husband – 3 trips to car 10:40/10:50/11:00, Mommy passes out 11:20-11:26, Mommy sits in back on two suitcases, 12 guests for late lunch, Uncle Fred & Aunt Helen, Mushroom & Spinach Omelets, Uncle Charlie & Aunt Betty, Coffee cake for 16, 8 minute nap, Mommy arranging dinner, Writing thank you notes while on hold, Cousin George & fiancee Estelle, Dinner for 18, Inviting UPS man for dinner, Putting needs of baby nurse ahead of yourself, Soy sauce & rice, Clean up kitchen, Letting nurse sleep through 10 p.m. feeding, Letting nurse sleep through 2 a.m. feeding.

Time Out

| 9:40 CHECK BABY | 9:45 FIND NURSE... ASLEEP | 9:50 GIVE BABY 10:00 BOTTLE | 11:00 GO TO BATHROOM | 11:20 WRITE FIVE NOTES | 11:45 SET ALARM FOR 2am FEEDING | 11:50 NITE-NITE!! | HOME |

Time Out

| 5:30 ADD DINING TABLE LEAVES + SET TABLE FOR (18) | 5:20 –DOORBELL– ENTER: COUSIN GEORGE + FIANCE ESTELLE | 5:05 GO TO BATHROOM | 5:00 HANG UP PHONE WHILE SEALING 10 THANK YOU NOTES | 4:38 WRITE 10 THANK YOU NOTES WHILE ON HOLD. |

4:37 CALL WING HONG WITH ORDER

| 4:09 PICK UP PAPER + PEN TO BEGIN ORDERING DINNER | 4:10 SNEAK PEEK AT BABY | 4:11 PHONE RINGS | 4:15 GO DOWNSTAIRS + ORDER EGG ROLLS + STEAK KOW | 4:35 CHECK WITH BABY NURSE FOR HER ORDER. | 4:36 ADD LOBSTER CANTONESE TO LIST |

Half Time |←Pass→|←Incomplete Pass→|←Offensive Push

| 1:35 12 HUNGRY GUESTS SEAT THEMSELVES AT KITCHEN TABLE WAITING FOR LATE LUNCH! | 1:30 GO TO KITCHEN TO MAKE COFFEE | 1:25 TAKE OFF COAT | 1:20 PHONE RINGS | 1:17 PASS WET BABY TO BABY NURSE | 1:16 GRANDPA PASSES WET BABY BACK | 1:15 PASS BABY TO GRANDPA | 1:02 FIND TWO SISTERS-IN-LAW TWO BROTHERS IN-LAW + IN-LAWS |

Flag on Play Time Out   TOUCH DOWN

1:00 FIND BABY NURSE, PARENTS + BEST FRIEND

| 11:50 LEAVE HOSPITAL | 11:52 DRIVE @ 20mph in RIGHT LANE | 12:05 GO TO BATHROOM NOW! DADDY PULLS INTO GAS STATION | 12:05½ DADDY PULLS OUT OF GAS STATION... YECH! | 12:10 DADDY PULLS INTO HOJO'S!! | 12:55 ARRIVE HOME! |

←Defensive Block

Time Out

| 10:35 HUSBAND SEARCHES HALLS FOR MEAL CART TO TAKE SUITCASES TO CAR | 10:20 HUSBAND COMES with DISCHARGE PAPERS | 10:11 GO TO BATHROOM | 10:10 NURSE COMES TO DRESS BABY | 10:01 HUSBAND TO ACCOUNTING TO PAY BILL | 10:00 HUSBAND ARRIVES | 9:33 FEED BABY |

Time Out   Fake

| 8:15 PACK SECOND THREE BAGS | 8:20 GO TO BATHROOM | 8:30 PACK THIRD THREE BAGS | 9:00 PACK LAST THREE BAGS | 9:30 BABY COMES FOR FEEDING | 9:31 BACK TO THE NURSERY TO GET RIGHT BABY |

89

The Game Plan
(Putting Together a Winning Strategy)

We know you're smarter than the Mommy in the Great Home-coming Game who, after landing on 93 squares, landed in the hospital. Take the time now to put together a winning strategy for taking care of Mommy beginning the first day at home. Start with a thorough review of the "Do's and Don'ts for Homecoming Day".

Do	Don't
Have your home organized, clean and ready for your arrival.	Come home to workmen. (This is not the time to change your pink nursery to powder blue!)
Have your husband bring the baby's bag to the hospital.	Have your husband bring 3 buntings, 10 blankets and 12 booties.
Organize yourself the night before: pack and send home plants and gifts in advance.	Wait until your doctor discharges you before you begin to pack.
Take home everything the hospital has "given" you: pads, toothbrush, etc.	"Borrow" the hospital linens or nightgowns. And no, the lamp and chair will not look good in your study!
Have your husband pick you up after he's installed a safety-approved car seat for the baby.	Put your tote in the car seat and tote the baby in your arms.
Say, "Goodbye and thanks", to the nurses, aides, room-mates (tears in moderation are acceptable).	Fantasize about relationships. You won't have time to lunch with the nurses, visit room-mates, or crochet everyone a "thank you" sweater.

Do	Don't
Invite your parents and in-laws over for a short visit and a peek at the baby.	Have both sets of grand-parents, all friends, neighbors, first and second cousins waiting in your living room.
Share the birth experience with interested friends and family. 	Give a blow-by-blow descrip-tion of the entire 56 hours of labor from your first contraction to your first hemorrhoid.
Write a few thank you notes, after you have rested.	Write for 24 hours straight to get caught up on your correspondence.
Organize yourself for the Birth/Christening, if it is to occur within the week, by making lists.	Spend your first six hours home calling the florist, moving the sofa, and booking "Franky and the Boys and the Band".
REST!	Try to run the stairs, run your errands, or run away.
Pay attention to signals from your body: an unusually heavy bleeding, cramps, fever, discharge, or red, swollen breasts.	Declare yourself "bedridden" simply because you've just had a baby.
Enjoy a delicious and favorite homecooked meal, prepared by friends.	Insist on preparing your family's favorite: slow-cook chili!
Record everything in your baby book.	Think it'll keep until later.

10 Things To Do for Mommy
on Her First Day Home

1. Set up the nursery.

2. Straighten up the house.

3. Place fresh flowers on her nightstand.

4. Allow her to nap.

5. Make formula, if not breast feeding.

6. Make the bed, including fresh linens and fluffed pillows.

7. Keep guests away.

8. Take phone messages.

9. Arrange dinner that night, including setting the table and cleaning up.

10. Draw her bath ... sitz, that is!

10 Things NOT To Do for Mommy
on Her First Day Home

1. Place a five pound box of her favorite chocolates on her nightstand.

2. Invite just a "few" close friends over to see the baby.

3. Tell her that he's "horny!"

4. Install another phone line in her bathroom so she doesn't miss any calls.

5. Inform her that his mother is coming for a short visit, three or four months!

6. Turn her "House Beautiful" inside out.

7. Tell her he's never seen her look better.

8. Cancel the help she's hired.

9. Change the baby's name.

10. Tell her he's exhausted.

An Old-fashioned Rivalry
(Siblings)

Homecoming is an especially difficult time for second-time Mommies, since they find themselves torn between the needs of the older child and the care of the baby. Four year old Becky needs to be reassured that Mommy will still have the time to draw her the alphabet during the day and draw her bath at night.

Mommy needs to be reassured, too!

10 Do's and Don'ts for
Taking Care of Mommy and Becky

Do	Don't
1. Give Becky a special homecoming present from her little brother, as you enter the house from the hospital.	Make that present a puppy!
2. Let Becky look at and touch the new baby before you turn him over to the nurse/helper.	Ignore Becky's need to check-out her "competition".
3. Maintain Becky's daily routine.	Overcompensate for your guilt by letting Becky "party" until midnight and sleep until noon.
4. Get additional help so you can spend time with Becky.	Use this time to cook, clean, or go grocery shopping without Becky.
5. Welcome additional distractions, such as Grandpa Joe and Grandma Ruth, to play with Becky.	Watch Becky play ... she's happy. You go rest!
6. Concentrate on Becky during the first few days and weeks.	Squander time that's for Becky by watching "All My Children", "One Life to Live", "General Hospital" ...

7. Slowly incorporate the baby into your lives.

   Take the baby everywhere you and Becky go!

8. Involve Becky in the baby's care to make your life easier: Becky will love running up and down the stairs for diapers, Desitin, and "Dumbo".

   Care for the baby behind closed doors. Don't shut Becky out.

9. Keep a stockpile of little gifts (books, construction paper, crayons, puzzles, paper dolls) on hand when company forgets Becky.

   Expect Becky to understand that she can't always get a present when her brother does.

10. Reassure Becky that she is loved. (Explain that Mommies are very special people because they have such big hearts that they can love Becky and baby, too!)

    Let your exhaustion keep you from taking the time to reassure Becky.

(**TCOM Prediction:** Mommy, Daddy, Becky and baby will live happily ever after!)

Instant Replay
(First Steps and Major Strides)

How many Mommies swear they'll never forget Junior's first steps, only to find out 22 years later that they only remember his major strides! Record everything, from the hospital to home, in the baby book. Remember, if it's worth a phone call to Daddy or if it brings a smile to your face, it's worth writing down!

10 Do's and Don'ts to the Perfect Baby Book

Do	Don't
1. Record vital statistics: full given name, date of birth, time, baby's birth weight and length.	Record vital statistics of the entire hospital staff that helped in your delivery.
2. Complete the family tree with the help of the oldest member of your family.	Use the oldest member of your family if she insists your Grandpa Charlie is really your Uncle Fred.

3. Save the newspaper from the day the child was born.

Save the grocery fliers with the specials of the week.

4. Save all birth announcements, including newspaper clippings.

Save the special chocolate cigars with "Welcome Lenny" down the side.

5. Include Mommy and baby's hospital ID bracelets.

Have them reproduced in 14 kt. gold.

6. Tape all cards, telegrams, and contributions into the book.

Include anything green: cash, checks, or the photo of your face on delivery day.

7. Record baby's progress on a monthly basis.

Include a record of his poops, pee-pees, and plops!

8. Include baby's birth picture and pictures taken in hospital.

Include the pictures of the newly remodeled cafeteria.

9. Include Brith and Christening momentos.

Press the leftover fruit or flowers into your keepsake album.

10. Record all gifts received, including check marks for each acknowledgement.

Rely upon your memory to keep track of who bought what, where, when, and why.

The Pep Talk
(Welcome to the Club!)

You've made it through the first day of initiation and you're now on your way toward becoming a "member in good standing" for life. It will take time to learn the rules, understand the procedures, and be a comfortable equal with all of the members.

There will be days when you will feel frustrated and will contemplate resigning, but relax—we know you'll meet *your* expectations.

Though the dues may be steep during the early years, we guarantee you'll reap wonderful rewards later in life.

Welcome to the club, and welcome home!

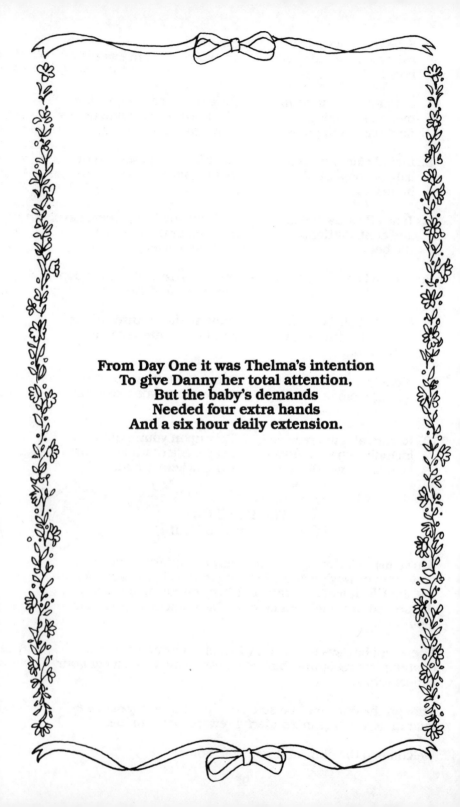

From Day One it was Thelma's intention
To give Danny her total attention,
But the baby's demands
Needed four extra hands
And a six hour daily extension.

Mommy's Daily Schedule

Dancing as Fast as She Can

"So, honey ... what did you do all day?" Nothing makes a new Mommy cringe more quickly than the sound of those infamous little words. And there's nothing more frustrating than finding yourself unshowered in your nightgown at 6 P.M. with your beds unmade, notes unwritten, and your husband's favorite chicken cacciatore undefrosted.

Whether you're a Mommy for the first, second or third time, you're never prepared for the time demands a baby places on your daily schedule. It's continuous, and it's overwhelming. (" ... and Betty told me the third child really doesn't make a difference ...")

There's nothing more disgruntling than having your life center around the baby every hour, every day, and feeling trapped by never getting out of the house. (Lack of sleep thwarts even the best of intentions.)

Time to bring Mommy back into step and choreograph her "6-10-2-6-10-2" into a manageable routine.

6 A.M.: To market. To market.

Early morning hours are inspiring. Many a Mommy greets the day with good intentions of being the first one in line at the A&P. Why, then, does it take Mommy so long to buy a gallon of milk?

Take a trip to the market with Mommy and Billy and find out.

How Quickly Can Mommy and Billy Get to the Market

6:30 A.M.   Billy gets up, stays in crib and plays. Mommy thinks, "I better get to the market this morning."

7:30 A.M.   Billy, Mommy, and Daddy have breakfast.

8:00 A.M.   Billy has oatmeal all over the walls, his hair, Mommy...

8:30 A.M.   Daddy goes to the office.

8:38 A.M.   Mommy puts Billy into the tub.

9:15 A.M.   Billy plays while Mommy makes beds.

9:45 A.M.   Billy takes a nap.

9:50 A.M.   Mommy cleans up breakfast dishes.

10:15 A.M.   Phone rings.

10:40 A.M.   Mommy sits down to organize shopping list.

10:55 A.M.   Mommy makes salad, seasons pot roast and sets table for dinner.

11:15 A.M.   Mommy pops into shower.

11:18 A.M.   Mommy pops out of shower... Billy's up.

11:20 A.M.   Mommy changes Billy's diaper.

11:30 A.M.   Mommy returns to bathroom with Billy.

11:50 A.M.   Mommy and Billy go to kitchen to make lunch.

12:20 P.M.   Mommy cleans up Billy.

12:25 P.M.   Mommy cleans up kitchen.

12:30 P.M.   Mommy and Billy go upstairs to get dressed.

12:45 P.M.   Mommy gets Billy dressed.

1:00 P.M.   Mommy gets dressed.

1:20 P.M.   Mommy packs diaper bag for trip to market.

1:50 P.M.   Mommy and Billy enter market.

6 Steps Absolutely Positively Guaranteed to Get Mommy out of the House in less than Six Hours*

1. **Put Billy in crib for his morning nap.** (If Billy is coming with you, dress him before his nap; when he gets up, all you have to do is change his diaper and leave!)

2. **Take the phone off the hook or turn on the answering machine.** (No Mommy can tell her caller how wonderful her new baby is doing in less than 20 minutes!)

3. **Unplug every TV in the house.** (No Mommy can resist the draw of a magnetic talk show host!)

4. **Take your morning shower.** (But don't take in your mud pack, henna rinse, and pumice stone!)

5. **Put on makeup first and then dress quickly.** (Try to mentally coordinate your clothes and makeup while you're showering to avoid wasted time staring into the closet!)

6. **Grab your coat, purse, and keys.** (Designate a specific place where you **always** keep your car and house keys!)

*If Billy is coming with you, add 15 minutes.

10 A.M.: The Joys of Taking the Morning Shower ... in the Morning
Look what happened on the way to Mommy's shower ...

... put the baby down at 10 ... good! She'll sleep at least two hours ... oh boy! Plenty of time to do everything ... make the beds, straighten up ... shower ... dress ... breakfast ... hope there's time to finish Aunt Gilda's thank you note ... think I'll make the bed first (phone ring) ... "Oh, Hi, Mom ... yeah ... yeah ... yeah ... fine ..." ... ugh, it's 10:20 ... have to finish the bed ... flip on TV for company ... ugh, it's 11 ... I did it again ... I always "space" into Phil, John, Bob and Richard ... better hurry ... get some juice and rye toast (phone ring) ... "Oh, Hi, Betty ... yeah ... yeah ... fine ..." ugh, it's 11:20 ... I better get rolling ... (doorbell) ... oh good, the UPS man ... "Oh, three packages ... thanks" ... what darling gifts ... better record them now before I forget ... oh, better call Mom ... Aunt Ida didn't forget the baby after all ... "Yeah, I was really pleased she remembered, too ... okay, Mom ... talk to you later ..." ... better get in the shower ... hurry ... "Waaaaaa ... Waaaaaa" ... two hours gone.

This *is* one of the most frustrating experiences for all new Mommies. Many Mommies who responded to the **TCOM** Survey expressed difficulty in mastering the art of the daily shower during the first several months after childbirth. Here's a foolproof way to take your morning shower before it's time for dinner.

All new Moms worry about leaving the baby alone for 30 seconds, much less for 10-15 minutes, while they take a shower. So, unless you have another pair of hands in reserve, give these waters a test:

If the baby is napping: Jump in, lather up and enjoy. Feel anxious, do you? What's the worst that can happen? (The baby may cry for ten minutes.)

If the baby is awake: Don't throw in the towel yet! Instead:

1) grab your "Comfy Baby" or infant seat and buckle the baby in

2) place a rattle in his hand

3) set him on the bathroom floor, two feet from the shower

4) run the water and hop in

5) lather up and sing your heart out! (Between the soothing sound of the shower and your gorgeous voice, your baby will be cooing in tune or fast asleep!)

Knocking the Pitfalls out of Mommy's Daily Schedule

Lists are at the heart of every organized Mommy. Here's the **TCOM** simple, three-step plan to prevent Mommy from wasting all of her valuable time. Compile the following lists on a weekly basis:

List #1: **The Bare Minimums:** What absolutely must be done each day. (Make formula, shower, dress, make dinner.)

List #2: **Responsibilities:** What you'd like to get done each day. (Make beds, write thank you notes, marketing.)

List #3: **Pleasures:** What you'd enjoy getting done daily and/or weekly. (Your favorite soap opera, return gifts and phone calls, shop.)

2 P.M.: "The Snooze" vs. "The Soaps"

Many times it's harder to "put Mommy down" for her afternoon nap than it is the baby. Mommy feels that there is always something to be done and that taking a rest is not only unthinkable, it's irresponsible as well.

Well, what is irresponsible is abusing Mommy's body! No one can walk around in a constant stupor and still expect to "dance" from dawn until dusk. Sleep is crucial for a speedy postpartum recovery.

Once Mommy has enough sleep to function rationally and happily, she can organize and schedule this overwhelming period in her life. Therefore, when the baby goes down for his afternoon snooze, put Mommy down, too (at least until Mommy starts getting a full night's sleep).

According to the A. C. Nielson Co., close to eight million people participate in some form of "love in the afternoon" (on TV, that is), and most of those participants are Mommies.

Soap operas offer Mommy an "entertaining" break in the afternoon routine. (How can you ever complain about dirty dishes when Henry's life is in such turmoil?) But beware! Sometimes Mommy never hears the whistle blow to signal the end of this diversion. She sits down at noon with a cup of coffee and before she knows it, it's 4 P.M. and the day and naptime are gone!

It's easy to fall into the soap opera trap. Therefore, **TCOM** presents the Great Soap Opera Test. Discover just how "hooked" you really are on daytime drama. Fess up: are you more involved with Erica, Asa, and Raven than you are with Mommy, Daddy, and baby? Turn off the TV and take the following test to see.

The Great Soap Opera Test

Answer the following questions for as many soap operas as you can. In many cases there is more than one correct answer. No fair cheating! **Scoring:** Score yourself on the "buddy system." Call up your friend (the one who fills you in when you miss a show) and check your answers with her. If you both agree, give yourself the points. (Maximum: 100 points per "soap.")

1. What's the name of the town? (3 points)

2. What's the name of the town hospital? (5 points)

3. Who's the Chief of Staff or prominent doctor? (5 points)

4. Who's the town's prominent attorney? (5 points)

5. Who's the wealthiest family in town? (5 points)

6. Who's the "ex-hooker" or "ex-con"? (7 points)

7. What is his/her profession now? (7 points)

8. Who was the last person to have a nervous breakdown? (7 points)

9. Who was the last person to die? (5 points)

10. What was the cause (natural or murder)? (7 points)

11. Who was the last person to have a legitimate child? (7 points)

12. Who was the last person to have an illegitimate child? (7 points)

13. Who was the last couple to get married? (5 points)

14. Who was the last couple to "split"? (5 points)

15. Which male lead is the latest "heart throb"? (5 points)

Bonus:

Who's the proprietor/proprietress of the favorite eating place? (10 points)

What's the name of this famous restaurant? (5 points)

*Above 250: Addicted-Viewing Mommy
You're not surprised at how well you've scored. Your addiction is no family secret. You wake up every morning and count the hours until your first "soap" comes on. Your husband's been trained only to call you during the commercials and

your baby's been trained to sleep all afternoon. (The only thing you want for Christmas, your birthday, and your anniversary is a video recorder so you can watch reruns on the weekends.) If you're the Mommy who can do all this and get yourself and your household together by noon—perk your pot, put your feet up, and pine away. If, however, you're the Mommy who's still in your nightgown at 6 P.M., ordering the double-cheese pizza for the fifth night in a row, beware! Perhaps your addiction is at the root of your problem.

*(Above 350: If you've scored this high, you're undoubtedly watching one network's soaps while taping another's. Call our hotline immediately!)

105–250: Regular-Viewing Mommy

You can't believe how many points you've scored. (Don't blush, it's okay—you can come out of the closet now!) You've been loyal to one soap for years, although you've never had this much time to watch it. You now tune in 3–5 times per week. If you miss a show, you have a friend who fills you in. If you own a video recorder you probably tape the show. You've arranged your baby's naptime to correspond to the show's airtime. You make this, along with your other responsibilities, part of your daily schedule. You look forward to sitting down for a quiet hour with a cup of coffee and your latest after-noon "flame".

25–105: Occasional-Viewing Mommy

You know enough about the action to hold your own at a dinner party, but you'd never let it hold you up in your daily routine. If you happen to be home and you're folding the laun-dry or making dinner, you turn it on for a quick getaway to Port Charles, Pine Valley, or Landview. You don't go out of your way to watch it. You enjoy the occasional diversion and company, but you're not benched if it's preempted by the "World Series."

Below 25: Nonviewing Mommy

You don't watch the "soaps" because:

a) You're a full-time working Mommy.

b) You find more excitement and fantasy with a good book.

c) You're so busy keeping up with your own affairs that you don't have time to track somebody else's.

d) You just don't like soap operas. (Perhaps we could interest you in a game show?)

6 P.M.: The Dinner Hour
(The Horror of all new parents!)

The last thing Mommy needs at the end of the day is her baby "cranking out" just as she's trying to crank up enough energy to prepare dinner. But universally Mommies agree—the dinner hour is a horror!

Though there is little Mommy can do to eliminate baby's "fussy" period, she can ease frustration during this time by enlisting the aid of a "Snugli," a swing, or a helper.

"Dinner!" How Mommy and Daddy Eat

1. Daddy eats, Mommy holds baby.

2. Daddy feeds Mommy, while Mommy walks baby.

3. Mommy and Daddy eat, while Mommy feeds baby.

4. Daddy feeds Mommy, while Mommy holds her ears.

5. Mommy and Daddy eat alone, together, quietly, after baby is asleep.

10 P.M.: Mommy's Hour

The evening is finally here. The baby's asleep. You deserve a treat at the end of a long, full day. Make the last hour of every night "Mommy's hour"—a reward for a job well done!

- Indulge in a long, hot bubble bath; (optional) ask Daddy to join you.

- Cuddle up with a good book.

- Unwind in a favorite hobby: time for knitting, judo, or baking bread.

- Share some special time with Daddy: make believe, make love, or make the bed ... but, do it together.

- Relax with a special TV show or movie.

2 A.M.: The Late, Late, Late Show

The only words that can comfort Mommy at this hour are uttered by a sympathetic Daddy: "I'll get up tonight, honey, you go back to sleep!" If you're lucky enough to get this response every night, give this section to Daddy. If not, here's a survival kit for the 2 A.M. feeding.

Get organized: If you are bottle feeding: have the bottle prepared and ready. If the nursery is "far" from the kitchen, use ice buckets and a bottle warmer (or hot tap water) to do the trick. **If you are breast feeding:** you're all set.

Keep the lights low: change the baby, feed the baby, and put the baby and Mommy back to sleep.

Feed the baby **calmly** and **quickly.** Don't wake up yourself or the baby so much that neither of you can fall back asleep.

(**TCOM Hint:** Warm milk works wonders for Mommy, too.)

However, if you can't fall back asleep, here are some suggestions from the **TCOM** survey for "6 Things to do and not to do" in the middle of the night.

6 Things to Do in the Middle of the Night

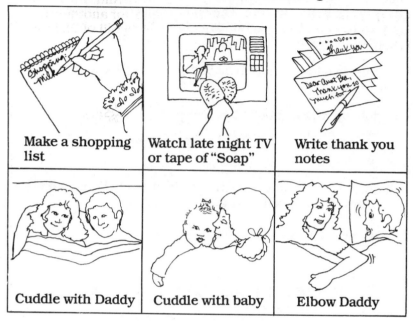

Make a shopping list	Watch late night TV or tape of "Soap"	Write thank you notes
Cuddle with Daddy	Cuddle with baby	Elbow Daddy

6 Things NOT to Do in the Middle of the Night

Vacuum	Cry	Watch Daddy sleep
Fall back asleep with baby in arms	Bake brownies and eat them	Make sandwich

When you're dancing so fast that you fall out of step, don't forget that Mommies have rights, too! Schedule the day to meet all of the demands, including your own. And, when you feel that you can't possibly do another thing for another living soul, sit the next one out and read "Mommy's Bill of Rights." (Then hand a copy of it to Daddy.)

Mommy's Bill of Rights

Mommy has the right ...

1. To be cranky

2. To be exhausted

3. To be comforted

4. To be pampered

5. To be put on a pedestal

6. To be appreciated

7. To be helped

8. To be left alone

9. To be wrong

10. To be counted

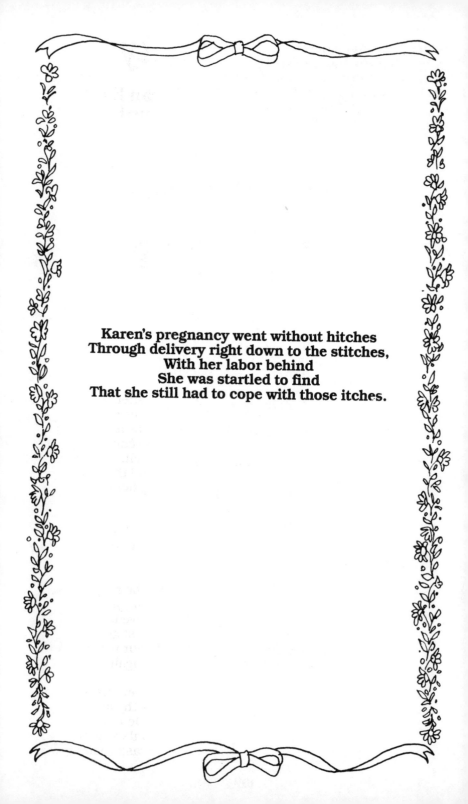

Karen's pregnancy went without hitches
Through delivery right down to the stitches,
With her labor behind
She was startled to find
That she still had to cope with those itches.

Sitting Pretty

How you and your bottom can live harmoniously after childbirth

Most new Mommies agree that "sitting pretty" after you have a baby is a lot like trying to sneeze with your eyes open: it's difficult and it's messy. Though not everyone has an episiotomy, stitches, or hemorrhoids, we have yet to encounter a Mommy who wasn't hit somewhere below the belt. While some mothers never give their bottoms a second thought, others spend every waking moment discussing hemorrhoids and "itchy-stitchy" with anyone who will listen.

Here are a few tips to help you during this time of recovery (usually two to three weeks). Follow them. And, in the end . . . you'll feel well.

Sit-uation #1: Re-toilet training Mommy. Don't be surprised if your first attempts at urinating end up flooding your hospital bathroom floor. Your bladder has been shoved, pushed, and stretched during childbirth. Now it, too, must get back into shape. Don't venture to the bathroom in your new furry slippers until you've mastered the basics once again.

Always rinse the perineum carefully with water everytime you urinate or move your bowels. (The perineum is the area between the vaginal opening and the rectum.) Do this conscientiously to ward off infection. (Most hospitals supply new Moms with plastic squirt bottles to make this task easier.)

The Mark of Distinction
Episiotomies

An episiotomy is a small cut between the vaginal and anal opening. Many doctors elect this surgical procedure to enlarge the birth ring and prevent it from painful tearing.

Episiotomies come in all shapes and sizes, ranging from *The Sampler* (three residents, two interns, one medical student stitching simultaneously) and *The Cross Stitch* (only done in parochial hospitals) to *The Double Cross Stitch* (done by the doctor who promised you anesthesia, but who made you "go natural") and *The Cable Stitch* (the resident does the stitching, the nurse holds the phone and the doctor directs long distance from Palm Springs).

Be sure to find out your OB's position on episiotomies before delivery.

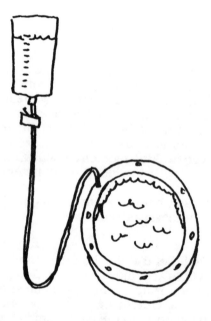

Sit-uation #2: Bathing Mommy's Bottom . . . The sitz bath. This is a marvelous and simple invention. The sitz bath provides welcome relief with constant, soothing, warm water. It is a bath in which your bottom sits (sitz). The most common type of sitz bath is a plastic bowl that fits inside your toilet bowl and hangs on the rim. A hose, which is connected to a bag and to the bath, continuously feeds fresh warm water into the bath.

Most hospitals provide a sitz bath kit to new Moms. But if yours does not, your bathtub will do the job. Just fill the tub with three or four inches of water, elevate your legs, and relax for 20–30 minutes.

Plan to sit in the sitz bath at least two to three times a day for the first week after the baby is born and once a day (or as your doctor recommends) after that until you're comfortable without it. Make this a relaxing time: read, write thank you notes, or even close your eyes.

Sit-uation #3: Diapering Mommy. After childbirth and continuing three to four weeks is a vaginal discharge called Lochia. This starts out bright red, gets darker brown, and gradually fades away. It is necessary to wear some type of protection during this time. Your best armor at the beginning is the hospital-size sanitary pads used by most hospitals. These stay in place (you must wear a sanitary belt), are incredibly absorbent, and are huge! We highly recommend you use them in the hospital and during your first weeks at home. As your flow begins to decrease, you can move on to the maxi and mini pads with adhesive strips.

Tucks, circular thin pads soaked in witch hazel to form a compress, are wonderful aids for sore stitches and hemorrhoids. Apply several Tucks to your sensitive area, "diaper" with your hospital-size sanitary pad and belt, and put on your comfortable maternity underpants. All this tender "luv" and "pamper"ing has you ready for Sit-uation #4.

Sit-uation #4: Putting Mommy Down: "Whoopsy-Daisy!" Move slowly. Think of yourself as a 45 rpm record, playing at 33. Though your mind is willing, your body may not be. Be gentle. No sudden starts. Or stops. When you get up, brace yourself on someone or something and rise slowly.

Sit on an inner tube (preferably one without Donald Duck or the Smurfs), a soft chair, pillows, or if all else fails, fold your leg beneath you. Make certain the seat you opt for has a back. This is not the time for the park bench!

Sit-uation #5: Hemorrhoids. Mommy's other little bundle of joy. If this is a new affliction for you, relax: worrying only makes them worse. It's all part of the wonderful world of motherhood.

Use the Tucks faithfully. Consult your doctor about special suppositories to help shrink large hemorrhoids. (There are a number of over-the-counter preparations that provide lasting relief.) Drink plenty of water (8–10 glasses daily) to flush out toxins and wastes and fight constipation. Use fiber or bran to reduce the discomfort of early bowel movements. Eat plenty of fresh fruits and vegetables to get your system back on track. (A note of encouragement: most hemorrhoids disappear by the time your real "little bundle of joy" sleeps through the night.)

Sit-uation #6: Toning . . . Kegel exercise. You are probably familiar with this term from your childbirth/Lamaze classes. This exercise restrengthens the muscles in the perineal area that were stretched during the birth process. Kegels are important for your gynecological health: they will improve hemorrhoids, stitches, and bowel movement, and aid in over-all toning of your bladder. (They prevent leaking when you laugh, sneeze, or exercise.) Kegels are also vital for happy, healthy lovemaking.

There's an easy way to understand the muscles you need to strengthen and how little control of them you have. Sit on the toilet. Urinate. And attempt to start and stop the flow. You can firm up (do Kegels) by tensing and relaxing these muscles.

Do your Kegels at least 50 times each day. You can do them anywhere, from the bedroom (during lovemaking) to the street (while you are waiting for the light to turn green). So, do them often!

Time heals all wounds. Sit pretty and wait, for this too shall pass!

Bottoms Up!

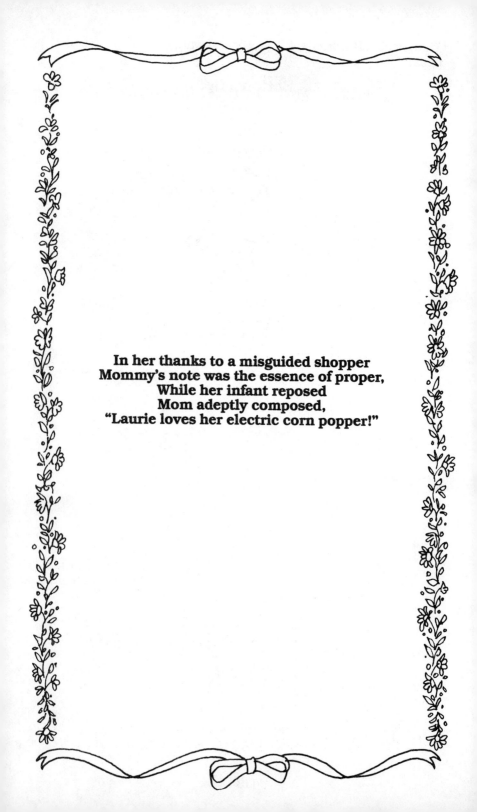

In her thanks to a misguided shopper
Mommy's note was the essence of proper,
While her infant reposed
Mom adeptly composed,
"Laurie loves her electric corn popper!"

Etiquette

Minding Mommy's Manners

You're 282 thank-you notes behind. The phone never stops ringing. Your mother-in-law's on her way over with her second cousin-once-removed for her 18th visit in 12 days. Before your exhaustion drives you to muzzle the baby and duck behind the sofa, consider these special rules of etiquette just for new Mommies.

Visitors

Rule #1: They should call you first

Rule #2: They usually ignore Rule #1

Uninvited Guests: Coping with Stranger Anxiety

While the last thing a new mother needs is unexpected company, it is one of the first things she always gets. It's difficult enough to make yourself presentable (without a staff of three) before 6:00 P.M. when you are expecting guests. It's hopeless when they arrive unannounced.

Both Emily Post and Amy Vanderbilt agree that it's "proper" to phone first before paying a call, but most people rarely do. Therefore, plan ahead so you don't get caught with last Thursday's roaster soaking in the sink or piles of dirty laundry heaped upon the sofa.

Handle well-meaning friends and relatives who "just happened to be in the neighborhood" by placing a note at the door, "Sorry I am unavailable now. It's naptime. Please call later."

Or, if you do feel like asking guests in (90 year old Aunt Sara who might not live long enough to make a return trip), keep the visit brief to avoid further exhaustion.

(**TCOM Hint:** If you make it known that you don't like drop-in company, you'll decrease the amount of "pop-ins" you will receive.)

8 Ways to Get Rid of Unwanted Guests

1. Faint

2. Fall asleep

3. Call the Orkin Man

4. Borrow your neighbor's dog . . . "Killer"

5. Cook cabbage

6. Eat cabbage

7. Break out the stale coffee cake . . . mmmm

8. Work on your "I Hate Unexpected Company" needlepoint

Invited Guests: The Welcome Sight

The recommended amount of time for a new baby visit is approximately 30 minutes. It's best to schedule no more than one per day, preferably in the afternoon. It's nice to offer something to eat or drink, but don't feel compelled to set up a hot and cold buffet.

(**TCOM Hint:** Keep plenty of paper cups, plates, and napkins on hand. Cheese and crackers, fruit, and coffee cake make good snacks.)

Little Guests: Seen, but no herds, please

It's not your problem that little drippy nose Rebecca has never seen a six day old baby. This is not the time to enlighten her. Newborns are particularly susceptible to illness. And you're particularly susceptible to being unnerved by other people's children. Encourage your friends to plan their first visit alone.

(**TCOM Hint:** Keep a supply of construction paper, coloring books, and crayons on hand for the "little darlings".)

The Peeking Syndrome: Visitors' Number One Compulsion

We say, "Boo!," to anyone who wants to peek at a sleeping baby, if "peeking" means "waking". And it usually does. Nary a visitor doesn't want to lift the covers to see new fingers and toes. Be selective! Let Aunt Sophie from St. Louis take a peek, but put Howard-the-Cleaners on hold 'til Friday.

(**TCOM Hint:** Pass out 8″ x 10″ glossies of your sleeping beauty instead.)

Delivery Men: Route! Route! Route!

This visitor is always a welcome sight, though his timing can often be improved. While you look forward to the presents he brings, his presence shouldn't be intruding.

(**TCOM Hint:** Post a permanent authorization note at your door so delivery people can leave packages without waiting for your signature.)

The Phone
(The Ding-a-Ling Dilemma)

Counting the rings. 1. 2. 3. 4. 5. 6. 7. 8. 9. . . . UGH! There will be days when you feel like pulling it out of the wall. Take it off the hook during private moments (showering, resting, time with baby and husband). Tell friends when it's most convenient for you to talk. (This is usually between 9 A.M. and 9 P.M. and *not* around naptime or mealtime.) Train your callers right from the start.

(**TCOM Hint:** If you can swing it financially, an answering machine is a great investment. Keep it set at four rings, so when you can't get to the phone the call will be answered automatically.)

Signing-off: "Ba-bye!" It's perfectly acceptable and understandable to cut your call short by telling your caller that you're tired, have things that need attending to, or that your baby's getting up. For persistent callers who won't let you off the hook, firmly but nicely say, "Ba-bye!" Click.

(**TCOM Hint:** In this case, honesty really is the best policy.)

Thank-You Notes
How to Write the Best-Baby-Notes-in-the-Whole-Wide-World

Step #1. Organization: Buy the book. Start by purchasing a good baby book. One with plenty of room for recording the gift, the giver, and your acknowledgement. Record *every* gift, including those you received in the hospital.

(**TCOM Hint:** Make it a habit to promptly record all gifts to avoid errors.)

Step #2. Picking the parchment: Bigger is not better. Many a mother has opted for the giant note in the shape of a teddy bear, only to pass out from writer's cramp before reaching Teddy's belly button. Unless you're a closet writer, resist the temptation to buy big. You don't want the size of the card or note to overwhelm your message.

(**TCOM Hint:** It's also customary to use your own stationery with your monogram or name on it. It's a social "no-no" to use Mr. and Mrs. stationery or your husband's stationery. Recommended quantity: begin with at least 100 and have a backup selection in mind should you run out.)

Step #3. Note Worthy: What and Whom. YES: *Contributions, *checks, gifts, flowers and visitors with gifts. NO: Cards, candy and visitors without gifts.

*Never mention the dollar amount of checks and contributions in thank-you notes. Tell the giver that the gift will be saved for the baby's college education.

If you get flowers and a gift from the same person, you needn't write two notes, provided that they arrive within a few weeks of each other.

What about people who say, "Please don't write us a note!"? Unless they are close friends, our advice is to write them anyway. Thoughtfulness is always noteworthy.

(**TCOM Hint:** People do understand how busy you are, but they are anxious to know their gift was received. Try to send your notes out no later than three weeks after receiving the gift.)

Step #4. The Bottom Line. Your signature vs. the baby's.

> "Even if the letter expresses the joint thanks of a couple, the letter should be signed only with one name ... the signer should refer to the other one in his or her comments."

Amy Vanderbilt

"The note may be handwritten, or on a thank-you card with a personal message. It should be signed with the mother's name, *not* the baby's. Everyone knows the baby can't say 'Thank you' himself, and cards that say 'Baby ... thanks you ...' are painfully 'cute'."

Emily Post

We agree. Pretending that four day old Lucy is writing the note isn't cute. In fact, it's annoying. Place your creative efforts in the substance of your note!

(**TCOM Hint:** Since it's so important and so often ignored, we think it bears repeating: ONLY ONE PERSON CAN WRITE A NOTE. ONLY ONE PERSON CAN SIGN IT!)

Step #5. Adopting a format: Prose and Cons. Every good thank-you note has four parts: an opening, a description of the gift, the intended use of the gift, and a closing.

The following is a format for thoughtful messages. Form your note with one selection from each category to create the best-baby-note-in-the-whole-wide-world.

Part 1. The Opening.

1. How thoughtful of you both to think of us during this exciting time.

2. What a wonderful time this is for us. Thanks for sharing in our excitement.

3. It was sweet of you to remember us during this special time.

4. I was so glad to hear from you regarding (baby's) birth.

5. Thank you for your good wishes regarding the birth of (baby).

(**TCOM Hint:** Try not to mention the gift in the opening sentence. Instead, thank the giver for his good wishes.)

Part 2. The Gift Description.

1. For clothes: Thank you for the beautiful blue romper. The yellow duck applique is precious and it's the perfect size for (baby).

2. For toys: Thank you for the Paddington Bear. The adorable animal will certainly provide (baby) with much fun and love.

3. For books: Thank you for the nursery rhymes and bedtime stories. They're a wonderful beginning for (baby's) library.

4. For strollers, buggies, etc.: Thank you for (baby's) first set of "wheels." I know we both will have hours of enjoyment from your wonderful gift.

5. For blankets, hand made items: Thank you for the gorgeous, handknit baby blanket. The colors are perfect for the nursery and I appreciate all the work involved. It's truly a gift of love.

(**TCOM Hint:** Try to describe the gift, including color and style. People are flattered by your attention to detail.)

Part 3. How you'll use it.

1. I can hardly wait until next (season) when he can wear your gift to (place).

2. Mr. Paddington is sitting atop the nursery dresser for all to see. Thank you for not only enhancing (baby's) room, but for giving her a new friend.

3. I can't wait to read them to (baby). And I know these terrific books will provide lots of enjoyment for us both.

4. It's perfect for both indoor and outdoor use, and (baby) will be comfortable as he's "strolled" through his early years.

5. Your beautiful gift will be displayed in the nursery at all times. And I know (baby) will be kept warm.

(**TCOM Hint:** Think of when and how the gift might be used. People really enjoy knowing they've made a good selection.)

Part 4. The Closing.

1. (Husband) joins me in sending many thanks for your thoughtfulness.

2. (Husband) and I appreciate everything you've done. Thank you very much.

3. Many warm thanks for your generous gift.

4. Thank you very much for everything. I look forward to your meeting (baby) soon.

5. Thanks again for thinking of us at this special time.

(**TCOM Hint:** Thank the giver again.)

10 Words or Phrases to Avoid when writing Thank-you Notes

1. Cheap

2. Ugly

3. Too big, too small or too bad!

4. So? Who would make such a thing?

5. The maid adored it.

6. Can it be returned?

7. I'm sure it'll grow on me. (If not on me, then on the floor, up the walls ...)

8. What is it?

9. I'm sure you meant well.

10. You blew it!

Gifts
"When they Care Enough to Send the Very Best"

We present, herein, the world's first list of the best, the worst, and the most unusual baby gifts, compiled with the help of **TCOM Survey Results.**

(**TCOM Hint:** Everyone remembers the new baby, but it's a special touch to remember the new Mommy, too!)

Great Baby Gifts for Mommy

1. Creature comforts: mani-cure, pedicure, facial, sauna

2. Sexy robe or nightgown

3. Cologne, perfume, scented talc

4. Instant Camera (loaded)

5. Books

6. Health club membership

(**TCOM Hint:** If you have a spa or health club in your community, check to see if they offer a special beauty package.)

7. Beautiful pen, notes, or stationery

8. Subscription to *Parents* Magazine

Great Gifts for Baby

☐ Sleepers in large sizes

☐ Baby toys, record albums

☐ White hooded knit sweater (perfect for all seasons: be sure to get large enough to last for 9–12 months.)

☐ Super coupe–deluxe with high back

☐ Diaper bag with changing features and washable fabric

☐ Books: nursery rhymes, ABC, etc.

☐ Musical animals for crib, buggy or playpen *NOT* playing "Brahms Lullaby"

☐ Car seat (safety approved)

☐ Playpen

☐ High chair

☐ Stocks and bonds

☐ Strollers

☐ Port-A-Crib

☐ Art for nursery: wall hangings, paintings, soft sculpture

☐ Rocking horse

☐ Record player (babies love music, and so do Moms)

☐ Needlepoint

(**TCOM Hint:** When investing $50 or more, be sure to consult Mommy or Mommy's good friend, especially if it's not returnable.)

Many Happy Returns
Not-So-Great Baby Gifts for Mom or Baby

☐ Baby clothes in small sizes (6 months size or less).
(If baby's birth weight is 8 lbs. or more, stick to
12–18 months size.)

☐ Baby clothes in large sizes (Toddler 2–4).
(There's no way of knowing how quickly your baby
will grow.)

☐ Using a popular store's box for an unpopular gift.
(There's nothing more frustrating than travelling across
town to one store only to find the giver's pulled a "switch-
a-roo" and purchased the gift at another store.)

☐ Personalized gifts that don't match or fit.
(Personalization, though darling to look at, should be left
up to the mother.)

☐ Anything playing "Brahms Lullaby".
(Because everything is playing "Brahms Lullaby".
Be creative.)

☐ Five pound box of mom's favorite chocolates.
(Truly the last thing a new mother needs.)

☐ Keepsake baby book.
(It's best if the mother can select the one which will work
best for her.)

☐ Baby blankets.
(Mommy always receives more than she can possibly use.)

☐ Decorations for the nursery that don't match the nursery.

(**TCOM Hint:** How to handle returns: Don't remove tags. Try to keep
everything intact in the original boxes. Be prompt. Always ask if you
can get a cash refund. (Many stores will accommodate your request
but don't publicize a cash refund policy.)

Baby Showers
(Tiny sprinkles)

If you're lucky enough to be the recipient of a baby shower,
sit back and enjoy it (along with the deviled eggs, the finger
sandwiches, and the punch). And remember to send out your
thank-you notes right away.

(**TCOM Hint:** Be sure to record your gifts in your baby book.)

Announcing The Birth
(Blowing your own horn ... properly)

Special Delivery: Birth announcements, like babies, come in a variety of shapes and sizes, ranging from the traditional formal engraving to printed helium balloons. Though Emily and Amy think that announcements come with no strings attached, we disagree. We feel announcements may be regarded as a solicitation for a gift and that they are best suited for informing out-of-town friends and relatives.

(**TCOM Hint:** If you do plan on sending them, save time by addressing and stamping announcements in advance.)

Blowing your own horn ... improperly

- Husband on rooftop with megaphone

- Air drop notices over your city and three surrounding counties

- Tell the neighborhood gossip

- Tell her it's a secret!

Religious Ceremonies (Brith/Christening)

Consult Emily Post and Amy Vanderbilt for the basics. Organize the following **before** you go to the hospital.

☐ Assemble the guest list

☐ Determine the time of day and what will be served

☐ Make a shopping list, based on your recipes

☐ Decide on rentals and/or paper goods (tables, chairs, dishes, silverware)

☐ Plan invitations: phoning vs. writing, depending upon your lead time

☐ Select an outfit for Mommy and baby

☐ Choose spirits: champagne vs. punch vs. sherry vs. wine vs. liquor

☐ Consider the clergy: who will preside and who will contact them

☐ Sweets: candy, cakes, nuts

☐ Flowers (optional)

(**TCOM Hint:** Get yourself organized in advance. Have all the orders ready to be called in as soon as you're ready to give the party. And don't forget to assign family members responsibilities.)

10 No-No's for a Brith or Christening

1. Hot dogs and baked beans

2. BYOB, BYOF, BYO ...

3. (Brith) Offering the Moyel (performs the circumcision) "a little something" to drink before the ceremony

4. Inviting your sister's husband's-cousin's-uncle (unless he's rich and generous!)

5. Calvin Klein diaper covers

6. Les Brown and his Band of Renown playing, "Hail, Hail the Gang's All Here"

7. Serving champagne with napkins from Aunt Martha's son's wedding

8. Distributing savings deposit slips

9. Your kid sister's rendition of "On the Good Ship Lollipop"

10. Howard Cosell commentating the main event

Thanking The Stork
(Gifts for the Obstetrician)

Though it is not necessary to give your doctor a gift (many think payment is enough), it does add a personal touch. (And it's a great idea if you plan on having additional children.)

Suggestions: (Price range: $10–$40) Pen and/or pencil set, golf shirt, sweater, or balls, decorative item for office, wine, something homemade.

(**TCOM Hint:** Send the gift to the office before your six week checkup.)

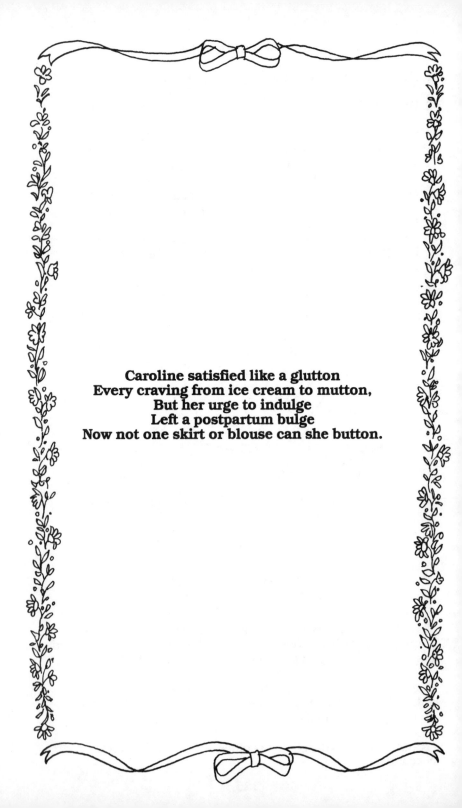

Caroline satisfied like a glutton
Every craving from ice cream to mutton,
But her urge to indulge
Left a postpartum bulge
Now not one skirt or blouse can she button.

Feeding Mommy

When the "fruits of your labor" are too much to bare.

There's good news and bad news about weight loss after childbirth. The good news is—you'll hardly have time to eat. The bad news is—even if you starve, weight comes off painfully slow. So, be patient. It took nine months to get to this state and it will take a good six to nine months to get back to normal.

With this in mind it's time to shed the "fruits of your labor" ... the **Taking Care of Mommy** way.

The birth of a thinner you begins in the hospital. There's no better time to begin a good eating program than after you've just had a baby. You already have a head start, depending on how long your labor was (eating in labor is usually a no-no, and we have yet to see a sweet table and buffet in the recovery room). Secondly, you already have lost a lot of weight just having the baby. And finally, you're not really interested in food, since there are plenty of exciting things to think about now. So, start right away and make the most of your hospital stay.

Talk to the dietitian. She will make sure you are on an official low calorie program of plain meats, clear soups, artificial sweeteners, and no hidden fats. If that seems too austere, then alter your regular trays so that they are more appealing and lower in calories.

Tips About Hospital Food

- Any item you write in on your hospital menu is going to have the added bonus of looking as good as it is good for you. ("Write-ins" are prepared individually and do not come off the line.)

127

- Every hospital has the following foods available on a regular basis: plain cold cuts, including turkey roll, roast beef, ham, cheeses; tuna fish in water; hard boiled eggs; cottage cheese; fruits (canned and fresh); vegetables without butter; salads; diet dressings; diet sodas; and so on. The dietary department of a hospital is like a grocery store.

- Hospital food is notorious for being high in calories. The cooks, though fine in talent, are heavy-handed when it comes to bacon fats, creams, butters, starches, etc. Hospital food is also much maligned. You'd be amazed at how appealing the peach cobbler and apple betty can be once they appear on your tray. Beware!

- The first trays you receive until your dietary requests are processed may look scrumptious and tempting. Try to control your enthusiasm. Save the quivering for holding your new baby—don't waste it on the hot roast beef sandwich with mashed potatoes and gravy.

- Most hospitals offer new Mommies a snack of juice and cookies around 8:00 P.M. Our advice is to become deaf at the sound of the bell or whistle!

- Ask a family member to bring you fresh fruit to keep in the room to calm cravings. (Suggested fruit: apples, oranges, tangerines, peaches, plums, nectarines. Avoid grapes and bananas, since they are higher in calories. However, they are still better than chocolate cake!)

- Remember: you are not using a lot of calories lying in bed. Therefore, though it may be tempting, try not to complete your menu plan as if you're seated at the 49ers' training table.

10 Ways to Keep a Good Thing Going:
Continuing at Home

1. **Begin immediately** with a sensible low calorie program, like the **Taking Care of Mommy Eating Plan.** A calorie is a calorie: it's a matter of simple mathematics. If you take in less calories than you use up, you're a loser (or in our book, a WINNER!)

2. **Learn to count calories.** There's no way around them. Those "high protein, low protein, high carbohydrate, low carbohydrate, high fat, low fat" diets are responsible for most of the "highs and lows" of dieting. It's a real high to lose the weight, but it's a real low to regain it quickly.

   Faddy diets produce temporary weight loss due to temporary water loss. They don't have lasting results. And the last thing you need now is to "yo-yo" on the scale.

3. **Buy a good calorie counter** and carry it with you at all times.
   (**TCOM Hint:** We recommend **The Brand Name Calorie Counter** by Corinne T. Netzer with Elaine Chaback.)

4. **Never get too tired, too bored, too hungry.** This is a strenuous and emotional time. Don't be too hard on yourself. If you fall off the wagon into the five pound box of chocolates, don't let the wagon go west without you. Climb back on immediately.

5. **Change your focus** away from food and "food for thought" producing activities. Don't watch TV if you can't watch a thirty second spot on Ruffles without ending up with the ridges on your thighs.

6. **Prepare food simply.** Read labels. Avoid salt. Don't fry. Foods should be broiled, boiled, or steamed without fats. Learn appropriate portion size with a good kitchen scale. ("Yes, Virginia, there is a difference between 4 oz. and 4 lbs.!") Chew gum while you cook to avoid tasting constantly (tastes have calories!). If the gourmet inside you suddenly emerges, poach fresh trout or sole and leave the Lobster Thermidore to Julia Child.

7. **Munching.** Keep raw vegetables sliced and clean in a crisper for quick snacks. Also, keep plenty of tomato juice or V8 on hand. *Don't pick up the baby's feeding schedule!* If you find yourself whipping up a batch of brownies for the 2:00 A.M. feeding, you're not focusing on feeding the right member of your household. Try not to eat between 7:00 P.M. and 7:00 A.M.

8. **Beware of visitors.** They can be fattening. When guests come to visit they shouldn't bring, and you shouldn't serve, your favorite coffee cake. Instead, serve fresh fruit, cheese, or vegetables and a dip. (You eat the vegetables and let the guests do the dipping!)

   This is the time to show off your new baby, not your culinary talents. If friends and family offer to bring you meals, try to graciously request fish or chicken. (Try to stay away from casseroles and lasagna. They may be easy for others to transport, but you'll be left transporting the extra pounds.)

9. **Baby's Leftovers.** Let them go down the disposal or into the garbage, not down you. Rice cereal and strained applesauce may not sound appealing to you now, but after 12 weeks on 1000 calories per day, they may sound like a gourmet delight.

10. **Dining out.** Avoid hidden calories: request salad dressings on the side (Ranch or oil and vinegar); food broiled, steamed, or boiled without butter; order poultry and fish; send the bread and butter away. (Recommended cocktails: white wine, tomato juice, iced tea.)

Taking Care of Mommy Eating Plan
Trimming the fruits of your labor
Paula S. Linden, R.D.

☐ Your objective is to get the weight off as quickly as possible. Slow diets encourage "yo-yo" syndromes and failure. Losing a pound per week might be okay if you have five pounds to lose, but it is an arduous task if you have 30 pounds to shed.

☐ There are no magical properties of foods or combination of foods. Ultimately all that matters is the total daily calorie intake.

☐ The foods to be eaten are divided into five major categories: meat, starch, fruit, vegetable, and fat.

☐ Begin at Level A (1200 calories) for 6 weeks. Cut back to Level B (1000 calories) for 2-4 weeks. Reduce further to Level C (800 calories) for 2-4 weeks and finish off with Level D (600 calories) to lose those last 5-8 pounds. (Note: Level D is a difficult level to maintain. Try it for one week or two. Take vitamin supplements and check with your doctor.)

☐ The amount of time spent at each level depends upon the amount of weight you have to lose and the amount of time it takes you to reach a plateau. Therefore, when you stop losing weight at one level, move on to the next. Use short-term goals for long term success.

☐ You may skip any or all parts of a meal and add it to another meal. (For instance, if you know you are going out, save as many calories as possible for the dinner meal.) Do *not* borrow from tomorrow's food (eating Tuesday's dinner on Sunday evening does not make for a slimmer you). You may not save from one day to the next.

THE LEVELS
(Note: Breast feeding mothers should follow their doctor's advice since calorie requirements are higher.)

LEVEL A (1200 cal.)	LEVEL B (1000 cal.)	LEVEL C (800 cal.)	LEVEL D (600 cal.)
Breakfast:	**Breakfast:**	**Breakfast:**	**Breakfast:**
1 meat	1 meat	1 meat	1 meat
1 starch	1 starch	½ starch	½ starch
1 fruit	1 fruit	1 fruit	½ fruit
Lunch:	**Lunch:**	**Lunch:**	**Lunch:**
3 meat	2 meat	2 meat	1 meat
1 starch	1 starch	1 starch	½ starch
1 fruit	1 fruit	1 fruit	1 fruit
1 vegetable	½ fat	½ fat	1 vegetable
1 fat			
Dinner:	**Dinner:**	**Dinner:**	**Dinner:**
3 meat	3 meat	2 meat	2 meat
1 starch	½ starch	½ starch	½ starch
1 fruit	1 fruit	1 fruit	1 fruit
1 vegetable	1 vegetable	1 vegetable	1 vegetable
1 fat	½ fat	½ fat	
Snack:	**Snack:**	**Snack:**	**Snack:**
Bonus	Bonus	No Bonus	No Bonus

The Food Categories

1. MEAT GROUP: 1 serving of recommended portion is
   approximately 80 calories. Do not add flour or fats. Bake,
   broil, roasted, or boiled.

	Serving Size
Lean meats (beef, lamb, pork, veal); trim all visible fats	1½ ounces
Poultry (chicken, turkey) remove skin;	1½ ounces
Fish—fresh, frozen, or canned in water: tuna, crab, lobster, salmon, scallops, shrimp	⅓ cup
Cottage cheese, low fat (read labels)	⅓ cup
Other cheeses, eg. mozzarella, ricotta, farmer's cheese, low fat cheeses	1 ounce
Eggs,	1 medium or large

2. STARCHES GROUP: 1 serving ranges between 70-80 calories.

	Serving Size
Bread—whole wheat, rye, pumpernickel	1 slice
Bagel	½ slice
English muffin	½ slice
Cereals—cooked or plain, dry or unsweetened	½ cup, ¾ cup
Crackers:	

Rye Krisp	3 triple crax
Melba Toast	5 halves
Saltines	6
Graham—2½″ squares	2

Rice, noodles, macaroni, spaghetti plain cooked (no added fat)	½ cup
Starchy Vegetables:	
Corn (frozen or canned):	⅓ cup
Corn on Cob:	1 small
Beans, peas, dried, cooked:	½ cup scant

3. **FRUITS:** fruits should be fresh, canned, or frozen **without sugar.**
   1 serving 40-50 calories.

	Serving Size
apple	1 small, ½ large
banana	½ small
cherries	10 large
grapefruit	½
orange	1 small
nectarine	1 small
peach	1 medium
plum	1 large
tangerine	1 medium
cantaloupe	1 cup
honeydew	1 cup
watermelon	1 cup
blackberries	½ cup
blueberries	½ cup
raspberries	½ cup
strawberries	¾ cup
grapefruit juice	½ cup
orange juice	½ cup
prune juice	¼ cup
apple juice	⅓ cup

4. **VEGETABLES:** 1 serving 30-40 calories.

Group A   Raw: 2 cups daily. Cooked: 1 cup daily.

asparagus	collard greens	radishes
beans, green or wax	cucumber	spinach
bean sprouts	eggplant	squash (summer)
broccoli	endive	zucchini,
cabbage	green onions	tomato
celery	lettuce	tomato juice
chard	mushrooms	turnip greens
Chinese cabbage	pepper, green or red	

Group B   ½ cup cooked daily.

artichoke	pumpkin
beets	squash (winter)
carrots	acorn,
green peas	butternut,
leeks	hubbard
onions	turnips

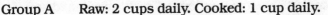

133

5. FAT CATEGORY: 1 serving between 50-60 calories.

	Serving Size
Ranch salad dressing	1 tablespoon
diet dressings (30 cal/T.)	2 tablespoons
margarine/butter	2 scant teaspoons
mayonnaise/salad dressing	2 teaspoons
cream, light or sour	2 tablespoons

6. BONUS: 100 calories

1 fudgsicle
1/2 cup ice milk
1/3 cup ice cream (10% fat content)
1 pudding pop bar
1 glass skim milk or 3/4 glass 2% milk.

7. FREE

artificial sweeteners
bouillon cubes
unsweetened pop
coffee, tea
salt, seasonings, herbs
lemon or lime juice
mustard

8. AVOID

sugar, candy, honey, jam, jelly, marmalade, preserves, molasses, any food to which sugar has been added, pie, cake, cookies, pastry, condensed milk, sweetened soft drinks, scalloped or creamed foods, the addition of any fats or oils to food.

The Telltale Signs of Needing the Taking Care of Mommy Eating Plan

- Your favorite prenatal layer cake has left seven layers on you.

- You're so out of control that you've just eaten the flowers in your hospital room and you're eyeing your roommate's roses.

- You can pinch an inch, you can pinch a foot . . .

- You believe, "When the going gets tough, the tough eat chocolate."

- Your idea of a "reduction" diet is petit fours, mini pizzas, and light cream.

- You're forbidden from certain streets during the spring thaw.

- At this very moment there is something fattening in your hand.

- You, your husband and your two best friends can't pull up your jeans.

One brief glance at her measuring tape
Convinced Jane she was quite out of shape,
To her utter surprise
She enjoyed exercise
Now the gym is her favorite escape.

Firming, Toning and Exercising

The Remaking of Mommy

Getting your weight back to "normal", whether it's 210 lbs. on a light day or 90 lbs. soaking wet, may or may not be a difficult task. However, in order to rediscover your 22 inch waist, you must participate in some form of postnatal exercise.

Ask your doctor how soon you can begin. Some doctors will advise you to wait until your six week checkup, while others will tell you to begin slowly, after the heavy, bright-red bleeding subsides. Whether your first workout is six hours or six months after delivery—stay in tune with your body. If you should notice anything unusual, *call your doctor!*

Grab your leotards and sweats ... it's time to work off Mommy's baby fat the **Taking Care of Mommy** way ... with a good plan, a good sport, and a good sense of humor.

Presenting ... The Most Recommended Exercises for New Mommies

1. **Chin Raising:** Lie flat on your back with your arms at your sides. Raise your head to touch your chin to your chest. Try not to move any other part of your body. Repeat several times. (This will help relax your upper back and neck and prepare you for doing sit-ups later.)

2. **Hand Clapping:** Lie flat on your back with your arms straight out at right angles to your body like a T. Raise your arms over your head and clap your hands together. Repeat 5 times. (This will help strengthen muscles underneath your breasts and improve the circulation in your chest and breasts.)

3. **Toe Pointing:** Lie flat on your back with your legs stretched out and together. Point your toes and hold to the count of five, then relax. Repeat 5 times. (This will help improve the circulation in your legs and is especially good if you have varicose veins.)

4. **Hip Rolling:** Lie flat on your back and draw both legs up. Keep your shoulders flat on the floor with your arms relaxed and out from your sides. Twist both legs together to the right, then bring them back up and twist both legs to the left. Repeat 5 times. (This will help improve your waistline.)

5. **Stretching and Reaching:** Stand up, raise your hands over your head and look at the ceiling. Stretch as far as you can up on your toes. Relax your left arm slightly as you stretch your right arm up. Alternate sides, stretching and reaching. Repeat 5 times. (This will help your waistline, too.)

The Great Burn-Off
Mommy's daily activities and the calories they burn
(Based upon Mommy weighing 130 lbs.)

Activity	kcal/hour
Changing diapers, sleepy baby	35
Changing diapers, frisky baby	350
Changing diapers, "dirty" baby	3500
*Carpet Sweeping	160
*Cleaning House	225
Cleaning house, with baby on back	280
Cleaning house, with baby on front	380
*Cooking	162
Cooking with one hand, holding baby in other	324
Dressing and undressing Mommy	98
Dressing and undressing Mommy while holding the baby	140
Dressing and undressing Mommy while holding the active baby	2400
Driving the car	78
Driving the car, while feeding the baby the bottle in the car seat	90
Driving the car, while feeding the baby the bottle in the car seat and singing, "Old McDonald"	110
Driving the car, while feeding the baby the bottle in the car seat and singing "Old McDonald" and keeping the beat with your foot	160
*Eating Dinner, seated	84
Eating dinner, while feeding the baby	204

*Grocery shopping	222
Grocery shopping during coupon week	444
Grocery shopping during triple coupon week	666
*Ironing	114
*Knitting booties	84
*Laundry—light (newborn weighing less than 7½ lbs.)	205
Laundry—heavy (newborn weighing 7½ lbs. or more.)	225
*Making formula	160
*Mopping floors	215-230
*Napping (lying at ease)	84
Rocking the 9 lb. baby	126
Rocking the 39 lb. baby	843
Running errands	216
Running away from the screaming baby	20,000
*Scrubbing floors	384
*Sewing (nursery curtains)	65-80
*Sitting at rest	72
"Sitting Pretty"	100
*Standing quietly	90
*Walking slowly, (2.6 mph), pushing the baby carriage	115
Walking slowly, (2.6 mph), pushing the baby carriage with a screaming baby	330
Walking slowly, (2.6 mph), pushing the baby carriage and holding the screaming baby	645
Walking upstairs	130
Walking upstairs to get crying baby (first time Mommies)	1300
Walking upstairs to get crying baby (second time Mommies)	13
*Window cleaning	210
*Writing thank you notes	102
Writing thank you notes to your mother-in-law	742

*Nutrition, Weight Control and Exercise, Frank Katch and
William McArdle, Houghton Mifflin Co., Boston, 1977 pg. 348-357;
all other activities are TCOM exclusives.

Ten Best Ways to Firm Up
TCOM Survey Results

☐ Postnatal exercise class   ☐ Walking

☐ Aerobic dance class   ☐ Tennis

☐ Jogging   ☐ Calisthenics

☐ Swimming   ☐ Jumping rope

☐ Cycling   ☐ Weight lifting programs

Turning Mommy into a good sport
(On your mark. Get Set. Go!)

From parachuting to shooting pool, Mommies are finding a sport, mastering it, and making it part of their lives. Approximately 50% of the 200 Mommies who responded to the **TCOM** survey indicated that they participate in a physical fitness program on a regular basis.

If you're part of the remaining 50% who's been sidelined, perhaps you don't know what you're really missing.

Here's a guideline to the eight most popular activities for new Mommies. They have one common goal: turning Mommy into a good sport!

Aerobic Dance Classes

(Note: Though not typically classified as a "sport", aerobic dance classes must be included here due to their current and growing popularity.)

Advantages: great cardiovascular workout (if class is 15 minutes or more); can do alone (TV shows or tapes) or in a group; terrific for the Mommy who loves to coordinate her leotards to her tights to her leg warmers to her sweatband to her belt ...

Disadvantages: not-so-terrific for the Mommy who doesn't like to coordinate her hours with the scheduled class hours; competitive; hard to be the teacher's pet.

Dress: Do's: brightly colored leotards, tights, unitards, and cover ups; Don'ts: underpants, support hose, hospital-size kotex.

Jargon: "Is she crazy ... she expects me to put what where?", "Uh oh, I think I pulled something!", "Help! I'm stuck!"

Cost: walk-in vs. class services; Danskin vs. Capezio vs. Dance Centre.

Calories burned per hour: 500-600

Bowling

Advantages: can play with three women you like and against four women you don't like; balls available in variety of weights and colors; you'll never work up a sweat; one of the few sports where participating and eating go hand-in-hand.

Disadvantages: does little to improve physical fitness; gives the average Mommy about three minutes of exercise; strenuous on the lower back; you'll never work up a sweat; one of the few sports where participating and eating go hand-in-hand.

Dress: Do's: consider Mommy's rear view, comfortable clothing, good bowling shoes, team shirts supplied by Harold's Hardware ... when free; Don'ts: rent size 5 shoe for size 7 feet, team shirts supplied by Shakey Shelly's Topless Bar ... even if free.

Jargon: "Can you bring me back a beer?", "Can you bring me back some chips?", "Where are we going to eat afterwards, Betty?", "Come on ... come on ...", "Move over this way" (hand movement to left), "Move over that way" (hand movement to right), "S---, that's what happens when you're up all night with the baby!"

Cost: relatively inexpensive if you're a light eater.

Calories burned per hour: 160-190

Cycling

Advantages: good for cardiovascular system; strengthens back and leg muscles; little trauma to body; scenic; can pedal with a friend; kicking level for stray, mean dogs; can take the baby with you.

Disadvantages: most people pedal too slowly for cardiovascular benefit; need a bike; restricted by weather; can take the baby with you.

Dress: Do's: pedal pushers, sunglasses, good shoes; Don'ts: bell bottoms, tight jeans, bathing suits, Dr. Scholl's exercise sandals.

Jargon: Feels like spring ... what a great day ... ugh, I hate this hill (pant, pant) ... (whew) glad that's over ... Oh, the Millers got a new car ... "Sit! Get away! Get away! ... ugh, I hate that dog ...", There's the UPS man ... maybe he's got that blouse I ordered ... what should I make for dinner ... ummm ... chicken ... let's see ... we had chicken last Wednesday ... that's a good idea ... good ... almost home ... there's the gazebo ... Gee, I hope the baby's still sleeping ...

Cost: price of bicycle, rearview mirror, horn, padded seat, rattan basket, light reflector, kiddie seat.

Calories burned per hour: 350-449, depending on speed, terrain, and type of bicycle.

Golf

Advantages: fresh air; good social sport; cute pro; can use a cart when not feeling up to par; great sport for Mommy to play with even-tempered-golfing Daddy.

Disadvantages: need a course; subject to weather conditions, bugs, allergies; white feet; low activity level; shortage of even-tempered-golfing Daddies.

Dress: Do's: short shorts, short skirts, short sleeved shirts, (little animals on left breast are optional), shoes with short spikes, short brimmed hat, short gloves; Don'ts: high fashion jeans, high hats, high spiked heels, Hy's gloves.

Jargon: "I think I felt a raindrop!", "Did you hear what Bill is doing to Sally?", "Did you hear what Sally is doing to Bill?", "Did you hear what Bill and Sally are doing to each other?", "What are you eating at the halfway house?", "S---, did anyone see where my ball went?"

Cost: public course vs. private club; cart vs. caddie; Mommy vs. Daddy.

Calories burned per hour: (walking) 240-320 carrying clubs and walking briskly; (cart) 185-220 per hour.

Handball, Racquetball, Squash

Advantages: conditions all major muscle groups of body; good cardiovascular workout if you're a good player; indoor sport for year 'round play; lots of courts; lots of A, B and C players.

Disadvantages: competitive; no cute pro; need to play on a regular basis; need lots of oxygen; when the courts and players are located three counties over.

Dress: Do's: see tennis and tone down; Don'ts: see bowling.

Jargon: "What's new ... how's the baby ... how's George ... did his Mom have surgery, yet ... any luck selling your house ... where should we go to eat afterwards ... I like your new shorts ... where'd you get them ... don't let me forget to pick up a carton of milk on the way home ..."

Cost: court-time per hour, ace bandages.

Calories burned per hour: 650-755 if fast pace.

Walking/Jogging/Running

Advantages: great for cardiovascular system; inexpensive; excellent release for tension; easy-to-learn jargon; can exercise outdoors at least eight months of the year; good way to meet the neighbors.

Disadvantages: doesn't build upper body strength; hard on back and knees; can get hit by a car; good way to meet the neighbors' dog.

Dress: Do's: elastic pants (most flattering), good running bra, good running shoes; Don'ts: drawstring pants (most unflattering), going braless, old "tennies."

Jargon: "You're running at a good clip!", "How far (pant, pant) y' goin'?", "Scuze me!"

Cost: free, or possibly, health club dues, orthopedic consultation.

Calories burned per hour: 500-800.

Swimming

Advantages: great cardiovascular exercise for legs, arms, back, abdominal muscles; relaxing; non-weight bearing sport, good for mommies with hip, knee, and ankle problems; don't need a partner (however, you should swim with a Buddy— Buddy Jones, Buddy Brown, Buddy Smith ...)

Disadvantages: need a pool; must wear bathing suit; must bare the "fruits of your labor"; chlorine burns your eyes; don't know any-Buddy to swim with.

Dress: Do's: Speedo tank suit, goggles, bathing cap; Don'ts: strapless designer suit, flippers, terry-lined shower cap.

Jargon: Hhhh. Hhhh. Hhhh.

Cost: health club dues, being nice to friends with pools.

Calories burned per hour: 350-420 if swimming fast.

Tennis

Advantages: great for body shaping, flexibility, and balance; singles and doubles games; indoor and outdoor courts; good social sport; cute pro.

Disadvantages: need a partner; need a court; need to play vigorously to get a good workout; need a racquet; need to know how to play; cute pro.

Dress: Do's: little tennis dresses, coordinated short outfits, sun visors, good "tennis" shoes; Don'ts: little tennis dresses in size 16, coordinated short outfits with balls stuffed in the pockets, PF Fliers.

Jargon: "S---, I keep hitting them out!", "Where should we eat afterwards, Amy?", 'S---, I keep hitting them out!"

Cost: court time per hour, 77 hours of lessons with cute pro.

Calories burned per hour: 330-440.

Source: **Rating The Exercises,** Charles T. Kuntzleman and The Editors of **Consumer Guide,** William Morrow & Co., Inc., NY, 1978.

The Great Health Club Test

From home body building programs to private spas, "health clubs" everywhere are opening up new vistas for Mommies, and more and more Mommies are opening up their pocket-books to pay for the privilege of exercising. (It is reported that three million Americans pay upwards of $300 per year to work-out ...).

Whether you're looking for company when twisting or looking for a company with a new twist, you should make sure you get your money's worth.

Take The Great Health Club Test and see how great your "health club" really is.

You know you've chosen the right "health club" if ...

1. **+10 points** The exercise rooms are filled with modern, easy-to-use equipment.
   +5 points if the staff shows you how to operate each machine.
   +150 points if Bruce Jenner personally helps you on and off.

2. **+5 points** They are open seven days a week.

3. **+10 points** They offer a "two-years-for-the price-of-one" membership plan.
   +5 points if you can pay in monthly installments.
   −250 points if the salesman resorts to high pressure sales tactics.
   +250 points if that includes deeding you his new Olds.

4. **+10 points** There are experienced instructors available to help you with all of the facilities.
   +4 points each: If they are sweet, patient, knowledgeable, skilled.
   +150 points if they are equipped with all of the above, plus big thighs.

5. **+3 points each** They have adequate locker room facilities, including: full-length lockers; keys on elastic bands; combination locks on request; plush carpeting; benches.
   +10 points if there are three feet between each locker.
   −25 points if there are three tushies between each locker.

6. **+25 points** They have accurate Health-O-Meter scales available to monitor your progress.
   +10 points if it's accurate to the quarter-of-an-ounce.
   −100 points if it screams, "Get Off You Fatso!"

7. **+3 points each** They take care of your creature comforts by providing: hairdryers; hair blowers; curling irons; plenty of outlets; plenty of sinks; locker room attendants; full-length mirrors; private dressing areas.
   +10 points if they provide makeup and perfume.

8. **+25 points** They have a pool, including **+5 points each:** olympic size; clean, chlorinated water; water temperature of 82°; a lifeguard; lane dividers; maximum of two swimmers per lane.
   +75 points if you can call in advance and reserve the "fast lane" for 2:15 P.M.

9. **+25 points** They have an indoor running track, including **+5 points each:** outdoor track, compressed rubber surface; good ventilation; comfortable climate control; piped in music; a water boy; 12-16 laps per mile; fast lanes, slow lanes.

10. **+3 points each** They have the best of everything, including: indoor/outdoor pool with underwater music; whirlpool; sauna with redwood benches; steam with minted scent; masseuse with registered hands; comfortable lounge; exercise room; treadmills; chrome-plated weights of various poundages; sun-room with automatic timer.
    −350 points if you have to pay an additional fee to use any of the above!

11. **+20 points** They provide regularly scheduled exercise classes on the hour, including **+2 points each:** prenatal classes; postnatal classes; continuous videotaped aerobic workouts; aerobic dance classes; slimnastics.
    −100 points if their celebrated dance workout is the 3:15 P.M. "Hokey-Pokey".

12. **+10 points** They have a comprehensive tracking system for your measurements, including **+3 points each:** using stretched-out tapes; allowing for "bloat"; whispering your measurements.
    −250 points if they dunk you in a "fat tank" to determine your body mass.

13. **+20 points** They have complete shower facilities, including **+3 points each:** hot, steamy water; soap; shampoo; conditioner; strong water pressure; large stalls with dressing areas; shower caps; paper sandals; talc.

14. **+4 points each** The interior of the club is: cheery and motivating; filled with lots of mirrors, watercolors and posters; accented with hot pinks and yellows; alive with plants, greenery; and six different varieties of ferns.

15. **+25 points** They take pride in the cleanliness of their establishment, including **+5 points each:** infection control team; mildew-free shower stalls, sprayed on the hour; fresh smell of Lysol and lemons everywhere.
    +75 points if the club motto is: "No fungus among us!"

16. **+5 points each** They encourage spur-of-the-moment workouts by providing racks filled with: leotards; tights; leg warmers; sweatbands; belts; tank suits; bathing caps; goggles; running shoes and socks; running bras; towels.
    +400 points if they whip out a rack of this season's newest fashions after you've showered.

17. **+10 points** It's within five miles of your house.
    +350 points if it's on wheels and it comes to your house.

18. **+15 points** They have a babysitting service on the premises, including **+3 points each:** a separate room; a-staff-to-child ratio of two-to-one; juice and cookies; the entire line of Fisher-Price toys; their own exercise room, complete with mini-Nautilis equipment.
    −500 points if you drop out of the "regular" club to join this one.

FOUR STAR: ☆☆☆☆ (Above 325 points)

Congratulations! You have a perfect "health club" in your own backyard. Since you'll never want to leave the premises, you'll undoubtedly look like Cheryl Tiegs in thirty days.

THREE STAR: ☆☆☆ (225-325 points)

This club might not provide you with valet parking or alfalfa on rye. However, it is a good, sensible place to shed postpartum inches, pounds, and blues.

TWO STAR: ☆☆ (150-225 points)

This no-frills club provides you with a complete body workout. While this club might not have a pool or a track, its positive track record speaks for itself.

(P.S. Remember to go home and shower before you meet your husband for lunch!)

ONE STAR: ☆ (Below 150 points)

Save your money! You're better off having your husband hold your ankles, while you do 50 sit-ups during "Johnny Carson"!

You Know You've Chosen the Wrong Health Club if . . .

1. As you pull up, you see the manager stuffing $100 bills into the back pocket of the county health inspector.

2. After you've paid your membership dues in full, you discover you can't fit in or on any of the equipment.

3. You have to circle the track 48 times to complete one mile (and it only takes you 38 times around your living room coffee table).

4. In order to get to your car, you have to walk through the neighboring ice cream parlor.

5. They take "before" pictures on Monday and "after" pictures on Tuesday night . . . the same week.

6. In order to swim you must take a number 2½ hours in advance . . . the good news is that there's a tin of yesterday's coffee cake to sample while you wait.

7. After four months the only thing you've lost is two pairs of Nikes, your favorite periwinkle blue tank suit, and the $300 membership fee.

8. Your mother-in-law belongs, attends frequently with four of her friends . . . and has a better figure than you have.

9. Their concept of "innovative exercise technology" is an old 10-Speed Schwinn up on a hoist.

10. There's a raid on the place and you're one of the 45 naked bodies tossed into the paddywagon.

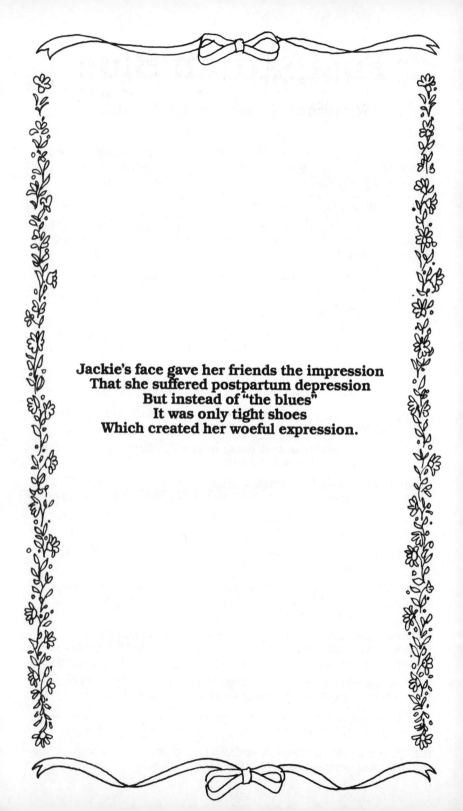

Jackie's face gave her friends the impression
That she suffered postpartum depression
But instead of "the blues"
It was only tight shoes
Which created her woeful expression.

Postpartum Blue

Mommy's Least Favorite Color

You need this chapter if . . .

- You think "postpartum blue" is a new color.

- During your six week checkup, you offer the doctor $20 not to mention it's okay to have sex.

- You're still eating for two.

- You're looking at the baby's warranty to check-out the return policy.

- Your husband thinks "division of labor" refers to the bylaws of the UAW.

  People are still asking, "when are you due?".

- Your husband thinks the "Mother of the Year Award" should be bestowed upon *his* mother.

- The 2 A.M. feeding means a snack to tide *you* over until breakfast.

- You still refer to your "new bundle of joy" as "it".

- The nurse is walking out the back door and your mother-in-law is walking in the front.

Life couldn't be better. You have a healthy "new bundle of joy" and the entire birth experience has brought you and your husband closer than you ever imagined possible. Friends and family are showering you with flowers, gifts, and love. Everything is perfect.

Why, then, did you just "knock off" the family-size Sara Lee banana cake, the half gallon of Fudge Ripple, and the two slices of frozen pepperoni pizza?

As you work your way to the spare freezer in the garage, you may be comforted to know that you are travelling a well-beaten path. Having a baby is one of the most physically and emotionally stressful experiences in a woman's life. It's exhausting and overwhelming!

This chapter will take you beyond classical definitions by offering simple explanations and a practical survival kit for taking care of Mommy during this awesome period of time, a.k.a. the postpartum blues.

Making The Diagnosis
("Mommy Sings The Blues")

Results of the **TCOM** Survey indicate that 71% of all 200 respondents experienced some form of the postpartum "blues". Their symptoms ranged from mild crying to feelings of helplessness. Some cases were so minor they went undetected, yet others were severe enough to require professional guidance.

Although many books have been written on this subject, we found the following description in **Our Bodies, Ourselves** to be the most direct.

> The first stage is the immediate postpartum feeling which we have during our hospital stay. We may feel incredibly high about the actual birth of our baby and tremendously relieved that there is nothing wrong with him/her ... and then we come down with a crash, aching from stitches and general weariness ...
>
> The second stage of postpartum, which may last from one to three months, is the actual coping with ourselves and our new baby once we get home. There is the incredible fatigue that comes from not having an uninterrupted night of sleep; the stress of incorporating this new person into our existing family; our changing role with our mate; along with our baby's constant needs. In addition to exhaustion, we may feel fragmentation, disorientation and chaos. Life seems a blur; we feel little control at the time.

Unfortunately, postpartum "blue" has an even darker side: postpartum "depression".

It takes time, energy, and good support systems to adjust to motherhood. If you're having serious and prolonged trouble coping, consider seeking professional help. (Your obstetrician, family doctor or friends are the best source for referrals.)

Charting The Symptoms
(Noting Mommy's Color)

Here is the first color chart of the shades of postpartum blue, Mommy's least favorite color. Which color blue are you?

Pale Blue: Faint, weak, emotionally drained; attacks suddenly when mother-in-law arrives at door with suitcase.

Light Blue: Mild crying, flickering on and off; rekindled by the 48th feeding in 36 hours.

Dusty Blue: Runny nose, itchy eyes; attacks four to six weeks after homecoming.

Sky Blue: Restlessness, desire to take flight; destination: anywhere. (Recommendation: See "Busting Loose".)

"Periwrinkle" Blue: Rapid onset; indescribable feeling shared after hospital discharge by those who "weighed-in" at plus 58 pounds and "weighed-out" at plus 60.

Peacock Blue: The type you're proud to strut! After 20 minutes and one good cry, they're gone.

Greenish Blue: Gastric distress usually following anesthesia, medication, or the 14th day of moo-goo-gai-pan.

Royal Blue: Soreness, chafing; associated with excess "sitting on the throne". (RX: Hemorrhoid ointment in queen size tube.)

French Blue: Desire, yearning, usually ending in frustration; when your mind exclaims, "Oui, Oui!" and your body proclaims, "Not me!"

Cadet Blue: Extreme exhaustion; comes on during your 33rd sleepness night when you're dreaming of sending six week old Billy to military school.

Slate Blue: Panic; feeling you get when the ballots are tallied and you realize you've just won a life term as "Mommy".

Navy Blue: Sinking, can't-keep-your-head-above-water feeling; creeps up during inclement weather when you're out of diapers, formula, and energy. (Recommendation: enlist some help.)

Midnight Blue: Drowsiness, spaciness; strikes after dark, usually during the 2 A.M. feeding; eased by dawn or a good "ham on rye".

Running The Course
(Following Mommy Down the Yellow Brick Road)

The Motherhood myth remains pretty much what it
has been for the last 30 years—variations on a theme
from "Father Knows Best", "The Brady Bunch" and
t.v. commercials for peanut butter.

The message is that motherhood is fun, easy, fulfilling,
natural, and the capstone of every women's life. Most
women, therefore, come to the state with rather unrealistic expectations of the sort of mothers they will be
and the sort of children they will have, without first
being given an honest job description of what they're
getting into.

How to be a Mother and a Person, too!
Shirley L. Radle

All new Mommies daydream. Here are the ten most common
fantasies of motherhood as reported in the **TCOM survey.**
We've added a dose of reality to lessen the shock!

> **Myth #1:**
> The Perfect
> Husband.

You have always known your husband was perfect. Why, you
don't need a baby nurse, you have Harold! He'll take complete
charge of the baby (not a fear in his body), so that you can
rest, relax, and get well fast. He's calm, cool, dependable ...
lucky you!

Reality: New Dads need time to adjust, too. They're tired and
going through many changes. Some are intimidated by a newborn's tiny size. Some are overwhelmed by the responsibility
of parenthood. Be patient. Help Daddy and eventually, he'll
be able to help you. (See "Coparenting".)

Myth #2: The Perfect Newborn.

Your baby will look like any one of the thousands of pictures you've been looking at in the magazines ... squeezable, pinchable, adorable, cuddly, soft ... and quiet!

 **Reality:** New Moms rarely know what a *real* newborn looks like. They are conditioned to motherhood by ads featuring "newborns". In reality they are six to nine month old babies who have just been fed, washed, and dressed. Don't be alarmed. Though your baby may look red, swollen, and dry at birth he'll have that "Gerber glow" in a few short months!

Myth #3: The Perfect Grandmother.

Your mother/mother-in-law will always be there with a smile and a helping hand. You can always count on her for an approving nod. And heaven knows, she'd never interfere! You always knew everything would be perfect once you made her a "Grandma"!

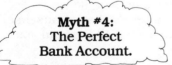 **Reality:** Mothers and mothers-in-law can be overbearing! Though they mean well, they can do too much, too little, do it only their way or not at all. Remember, this is also a thrilling time for them and they need your help to adjust. (See "Grandmothers".)

Myth #4: The Perfect Bank Account.

There's no need to budget now. You know you'll be showered with the gifts and money after the baby's born. Why, Uncle Fred's always been very giving. Aunt Sophie will "kick in a bundle" (even more if we name the baby after her). And the grandparents can't wait to spoil their first grandchild.

Reality: While friends and family may be generous, it's your responsibility to provide for the things you need. Your family planning should include financial planning. Don't make the mistake of depending on others.

Myth #5:
The Perfect
Homecoming.

As your husband carries you and the baby over the threshold, you'll enter into an immaculate home filled with fresh flowers and the warm aroma of your favorite roast cooking in the oven. The baby will sleep all afternoon and you and your husband will spend a relaxing first day together.

Reality: My, oh my! You come home to find people and chaos. (You never knew so many bodies could fit into your living room at one time!) The day is an endless parade of well-meaning friends, special deliveries, and dirty dishes. It's overwhelming! (See "Homecoming".)

Myth #6:
The Perfect
Encounter.

You and your husband will immediately resume your intimate, loving sexual life. It's always been perfect, so why shouldn't it continue to be? Wait six weeks? That's nonsense! How could you ever postpone making love with the man you adore!

Reality: Very little goes on in your bed other than watching TV, talking, and sleeping. Wait six weeks? Are you sure the doctor didn't say six months? (See "Sex. The 'R' Rated Chapter".)

Myth #7:
The Perfect Planner.

Motherhood will be a breeze! You'll be up at six, have the baby and yourself bathed and dressed by seven, go into your office for four hours, and stop off to get your hair trimmed while the butcher's trimming your roast. You'll cook your favorite dinner and have the champagne iced before your husband gets home. You'll share an intimate (and uninterrupted) evening together.

Reality: You have a headache that won't quit! The baby cried for seven hours, you've done three loads of laundry, made two batches of formula, written 22 thank you notes, and walked, rocked, and sang. Cook dinner? You sure have high hopes! (See "Mommy's Daily Schedule".)

Myth #8:
The Perfect Silhouette.

What amazing willpower you'll have. You'll spend three weeks eating cottage cheese, string beans, and lettuce and doing 85 sit-ups everyday, and then you'll be back to your pre-pregnancy state. In fact, you'll look even better than before. (Losing 30 pounds won't be bad at all.)

Reality: It takes lots of hard work and perseverance to get back into shape, usually six to nine months. Be patient! (See "Feeding Yourself" and "Firming Yourself".)

Myth #9:
The Perfect
Night Feeding.

You just can't understand why your friends complain about the 2 A.M. feeding. You're looking forward to a few quiet moments alone with the baby during this peaceful time. (Besides, you know he'll only get up once, you'll quickly change and feed him and return to your dreams in 20 minutes.)

Reality: Sammy screams at 11, at 3, and at 5 A.M.; six hours, five diapers and four feedings later, you finally get him settled in for the night. Just as you crawl into bed, the alarm clock rings.

Myth #10:
The Perfect
Postpartum Blues.

You don't know what all the fuss is about. "A depression that hits after the baby's born?" Humph. You've waited seven long years for this healthy, sweet little bundle. How could it ever bring a tear to your eye! "Emotionally and physically drained?" Why, between your husband, mother, mother-in-law, and Aunt May, you'll have plenty of time to rest.

Reality: This fantasy can come true if you take the time to understand the common myths of motherhood. A realistic attitude and realistic expectations can help you "waltz" your blues away!

Recommended Therapy
(TCOM Survival Kit)

Ten Great Ways to Muddle Through the Postpartum Blues

1. **Go on a shopping spree.** Buy something wonderful ... and extravagant!

2. **Have lunch with a friend.** Discuss everything ... except the new baby!

3. **Eat right.** Resist the temptation to drown your sorrows in a hot fudge sundae ... start a sensible eating plan!

4. **Borrow a close shoulder.** Lean on it ... or have a good cry!

5. **Start exercising (with your doctor's permission.)** Work out your frustration and tension ... work off your hips and thighs.

6. **Make time for Mommy.** Pick your favorite passion, (knitting, sewing, reading,) and take an hour's vacation each day from the overwhelming state of motherhood.

7. **Rest.** Take a nap ... you'll have a better grasp on life when you're well-rested! (Things really do look better in the morning.)

8. **Hire additional help.** Plan a special outing on a regular basis ... without the baby!

9. **Escape with Daddy.** Treat yourselves to a "night on the town" ... often!

10. **Pamper yourself.** Unwind in a manicure, pedicure, facial, or massage ... you'll look great and feel great, too!

Final Prognosis
(Color Mommy ... Healthy!)

You now have a clear perspective of the postpartum blues— their range of shades, the course they run, and the best plan for management (survival kit).

Remember, the "blues" handle everyone (or everyone handles them) differently. Rely on time, close friends, and this chapter to "cure" yours with nary a ruffle. Here's to a case of the peacock blues!

On their first dinner outing alone
Tom could not keep his wife from the phone,
With a purse full of dimes
Ann called home 16 times
Just between her pea soup and T-bone.

Guilt, Anxieties ... and Fears

The Other Side of Midnight

Who'd have thought that when your sister-in-law told you this would be a "trying time", she meant your performance as a Mommy would be constantly on trial. Even the most secure Mommies can't escape the pressure of the daily or weekly verdict. And the accompanying judgments made by others and Mommy, too: "Am I really doing the right thing by going back to work?" (guilt) "Am I capable of being a good Mommy?" (anxiety) "Will I ever be able to change a dirty diaper without gasping?" (fear)

(And you thought all you were getting in the delivery room was an 8 lb. 3 oz. "bundle of joy". Little did you know that you were also getting bundles of guilt, anxieties ... and fears.)

Some Mommies spend their entire lives waiting for an acquittal while others find the self-assurance to dismiss the jury at the start. Yet, all Mommies will agree, at times advice can be consoling, but it must be combined with a big dose of self-confidence and a lot of "I am going to be a good Mommy" to dissipate guilt, anxieties ... and fears.

(**TCOM Hint:** If you find your guilt, anxieties ... and fears getting stronger with time instead of lessening, you may want to consider professional help.)

Part One: Guilt

Guilt is the feeling you get when you express the way you feel ("Gee, I'd really like to put my feet up and read the paper") and combine it with the way you were programmed to feel ("Work before Play").

Guilt can be "inflicted" by others or it can be self-imposed. While guilt cannot be prevented, its intensity can be controlled. Hence, **TCOM's** "Guilt Grid", the five most common guilts and their five most common guilt givers (according to **TCOM** Survey results).

	Guilt #1: **Making Time For Daddy**	Guilt #2: **Making Time for Other Children**
Your heart says	"I should force myself to play Boggle with Daddy even though I'm so exhausted."	"I should force myself to spend as much time as possible with my older child, who really needs me now."
Your mind says	"Game of Boggle ... that's fine, but let him take the 2 A.M. feeding."	"If I don't get grandma in here to play with Beth, I'm going to collapse from exhaustion."
Daddy says	"Can't you ever make time for me? I need to be with you alone."	"Don't tell me you spent the whole day playing with the kids?"
Mom/Mother-in-law says	"Remember Harold, dear—you shouldn't neglect him."	"I know the baby's only six weeks old, dear—but don't you think he needs a little more attention?"
Your friend says	"If my David was as sweet as your Phil, I certainly wouldn't complain about making time for him."	"I know you just had a baby two weeks ago, but don't you think you should come to the play group with Beth?"
Your baby "says"	"I need you."	"I need you."

Guilt #3: **Making Time For Mommy**	*Guilt #4: **Returning To Work**	Guilt #5: **Breast vs. Bottle**
"I should force myself to take a bubble bath, read the paper and relax—an hour for me."	"I should force myself to stay home with the kids—I can never find childcare that can give them what I can."	"I should force myself to breast feed—there's nothing more beautiful, healthy and natural."
"Relax? The sink is filled with dishes, the washing machine's filled with diapers and the living room is filled with toys."	"We really need the extra income and I really need the adult stimulation."	"I just really don't want to."
"Funny how you can find time for a bubble bath, but you can't sit down to talk with me."	"On one hand we need the money, on the other hand the baby needs you. On one hand you need the fulfillment, on the other hand …"	"I think you should."
"When I was your age, dear-we would never think of leaving the house before the beds were made and the dishes done."	"You really should stay home with the kids until they're in school, dear—I don't care what those studies say, the children will suffer."	"I suppose you know what's best, dear?"
"Gee, I wish I could have taken the time off to exercise when I had all those notes to write."	"I suppose you know what you're doing, but I don't know anybody who went back to work quite so soon."	"I suppose you should do what you want, but I could never do that!"
"I need you."	"I need you."	"I need you."

Part Two: Anxiety

Anxiety is the uncomfortable and stressful feeling about a future uncertainty (motherhood). Anxiety runs the gamut from five minutes of uneasiness when the new sitter walks through the front door to a full-blown anxiety "attack" (sweaty palms, fast pulse, shortness of breath, stomach distress) rendering you out of control.

The following are illustrations of common motherhood anxieties, accompanied by some "tried-and-true" methods for controlling them.

Anxieties-All-New-Mothers-Have-At-One-Time-Or-Another-But-Are-Afraid-To-Acknowledge

The Anxiety about Motherhood

Mommy is thrilled with the baby, but feels anger and guilt about all the time and work involved in just caring for the child ... Everyone has a difficult time! But hardly anyone admits it or admits the depth and extent of their feelings. This can isolate us even more and make us feel inadequate.

Motherhood, The First 12 Months
Deborah Insel

The Top 10 Things 200 Mommies Stated Were Worthy of an Anxiety "Attack" (TCOM Survey Results)

- **Anxiety of failure** "Am I really cut out to be a good Mommy?" "Did I make a mistake by having this baby?"

- **Anxiety of incompetence** "What happens if I do something accidentally that harms the baby?" "Will I always be able to think clearly?"

- **Anxiety of not being able to cope** "When the baby cries nonstop, I feel so helpless."

- **Anxiety of the marital relationship changing** "When will I find the time and energy to be alone with Robert?" "Why can't Robert see that the baby's needs have to come first now?"

- **Anxiety of breast feeding** "Is the baby getting enough milk?" "What if I fall asleep during the middle of the night feeding?" "How can I breast feed in public? I'm so self-conscious."

- **Anxiety of baby's health** "What will I do when the baby vomits?"
  "What happens if the baby gets diaper rash?"
  "What if the belly button gets infected?"

- **Anxiety of first bath** "What if the baby slips out of my hands?"
  "How can I wash the baby and hold him at the same time?"
  "Where am I going to give the baby a bath?"

- **Anxiety of sibling rivalry** "What if Amy tries to harm the baby?"
  "What if Amy can't adjust?"
  "How will I satisfy both sets of needs?"

- **Anxiety of baby's weight gain** "Is he gaining too much?"
  "Is he gaining too little?"
  "Am I overfeeding?"
  "Am I starving him?"

- **Anxiety of Mommy's weight gain** "I can't believe I have so much weight to lose."
  "It's so hard to diet when I'm up around-the-clock."

The Advice 200 Mommies Gave for Dealing with Their Anxieties (TCOM Survey Results)

- Take one day at a time.

- Read everything on motherhood.

- Talk to other mothers.

- Rely upon your common sense.

- Talk with your husband.

- Talk with your pediatrician.

- Invest the time to find a good sitter.

- Trust your instincts.

- Be flexible and adapt to change.

- Use your sense of humor.

- Be patient and allow time to work its magic.

OTHERS OPINIONS

MOMMY'S STANDARDS

The Top 10 Things 200 Mommies Stated Were Not Worthy of an Anxiety "Attack"
(TCOM Survey Results)

Messy House

Making Dinner

Losing Weight Fast Enough

Laundry Build-up

Writing Thank You Notes

Hair Falling Out

Not Getting Dressed

Drop-in Company

Baby Off Schedule

Looking Good All The Time

Flying Solo
The Anxiety of Stepping Out Without the Baby

Mommy may be so preoccupied with the baby that when she does "fly solo", she spends most of the time thinking about what's going on at home. She may be concerned that no one else can care for the baby like a mother can. And she feels anxious putting this "theory" to the test.

While many first-time Mommies have an especially difficult time dealing with the separation, this anxiety tends to decrease with subsequent births.

Though it may take several outings before Mommy will be comfortable leaving the baby, the following plan will help lessen the initial anxiety and encourage a solo flight before Annie reaches kindergarten.

The TCOM Separation Anxiety Reduction Plan
"A No-Sweat Guide to Getting Away"

1. **Leave the baby with a trustworthy, loving caregiver ... Grandma or a close friend is ideal.** When Mommy really believes that the baby is in great hands, she can relax and enjoy her free time away.

   TCOM Survey Results: "Who babysat during your first outing without the baby?"

49%	mother	15%	nurse
24%	babysitter	12%	good friend

2. **Stay away as long as you feel comfortable.** Trust your instincts, and return home when you feel the desire. (And, don't go to dinner at a restaurant that has slow service on your first outing out!)

   TCOM Survey Results: "How long were you gone on your first outing?"

   3 hours (average)

3. **Plan something just for you.** You'll be able to cope with your first outing more easily if you're doing something you really enjoy.

   TCOM Survey Results: "Where did you go on your first outing?"

   44%   Out to dinner with Daddy
   32%   Shopping
   12%   Movies
   12%   Party

4. **Call home as often as you feel the need.** Checking in reduces anxiety.

   TCOM Survey Results: "How many times did you call home?"

   42%   None
   46%   Once
   11%   Twice
    2%   Three Times

5. **"Fly solo" as soon as you feel the urge, whether it's the first week or the first month.** And do it on a continuing basis. Don't forget the importance of taking care of Mommy, too.

Keeping Up with the Jones' Baby
The Anxiety of Comparing Your Child to Your Friend's

This is one of the major afflictions of first-time Mommies that develops into a chronic condition with each subsequent birth. Mommy seems to have a need to chart her child's progress against that of her neighbor's: "How old was Joanie when she turned, rolled over, crawled, stood, said "Da Da", and walked?"

Mommy is comforted when she discovers her little Annie is more advanced than the competition. However, if the reverse occurs and Annie turns out to be "behind" Joanie, Mommy may thrust herself into an anxiety "attack".

All Mommies compare their children's progress to others. The key is to minimize the importance Mommy places on the results. If you're well-acquainted with the normal ranges of development, you won't be thrown into a "tizzy" if you find your child at one end or the other of the Jones' yardstick. (See "Packing Mommy's Head" for reading suggestions.)

(**TCOM Hint:** Check it out of the library before you check it out with your friends. If you don't think your child is advancing quickly enough call your pediatrician, not Mrs. Jones!)

Part Three . . . and Fears

Fear is a feeling of alarm caused by a specific threat. While new Mommies are filled with a lot of real fears (many of which were discussed earlier), here are some not-so-real fears all Mommies share and can laugh about, together.

(**TCOM Hint:** If you find your fears are unmanageable and are becoming phobias, consult professional help.)

TCOM's Common "Fears" of Motherhood

Asthenophobia (fear of weakness): Descends upon Mommy on day three of dieting; convinces Mommy that if she doesn't eat a Snickers bar within 60 seconds she'll pass out from malnutrition. (Rx: Glass of skim milk)

Onomotophobia (fear of name): Overcomes Mommy in the eighth month when Daddy suggests that if the baby's a girl, she be named after his favorite grandmother, Bertha. (Rx: Have a boy)

Kinesophobia (fear of motion): Grabs Mommy suddenly in the middle of the night after one hour of trying to rock the baby to sleep ... unsuccessfully. (Rx: Dramamine)

Graphophobia (fear of writing): Begins with tightening of the finger muscles and progresses to inability to use writing hand; brought about by writing 112 thank you notes in six days. (Rx: 112 thank you notes in 12 days)

Hodophobia (fear of travel): Surrounds Mommy during the planning of the "first getaway" when Mommy wants romance and Daddy wants adventure; often results in Mommy ending up in the Poconos and Daddy ending up in the Chatahoochee River. (Rx: The Great Getaway Test)

Zoophobia (fear of animals): Hits Mommy somewhere between purchasing the tenth stuffed goose in her ninth month and receiving the seventeenth Paddington Bear after the baby's born. (Rx: Paddington Bears make wonderful Christmas, Homecoming, new office and welcoming gifts)

Neophobia (fear of anything new): Pounces upon Mommy in the ninth month when the layette is delivered; compels Mommy to wash everything six times on the gentle cycle with baby soap, baby booster, and baby softener. (Rx: Help from grandma)

Patriophobia (fear of heredity): Creeps up in the second trimester during a long walk when Mommy and Daddy re-discover each other: "Walter, I didn't know you had your ears pinned back ...", "Carol, I didn't know you had a birthmark there ..." (Rx: Keep digging to discover the "blossoms" on your family tree)

Genophobia (fear of sex): Prevails in Mommies who received 15 or more episiotomy stitches; causes Mommy to proceed with caution even after the "light turns green". (Rx: A gallon of K-Y jelly)

Osmophobia (fear of odor): Strikes Mommy usually after naptime when the scent from the baby's room can be detected three doors down. (Rx: Super strength, lemon scented Triple-X Air Freshner)

Microphobia (fear of small objects): Invades Mommy the moment the baby begins to crawl; forces Mommy to remove everything smaller than a bread box from the baby's reach. (Rx: Shelves five feet high and above)

Xenophobia (fear of strangers): Attacks Mommy in the hospital when she is examined by everyone except her own OB; intensifies after delivery when Mommy is taken to a ward. (Rx: Home delivery)

When the going gets rough and Daddy comes home and finds you huddled in the corner crying, hand him this page.

Interpreting Mommy's Cries

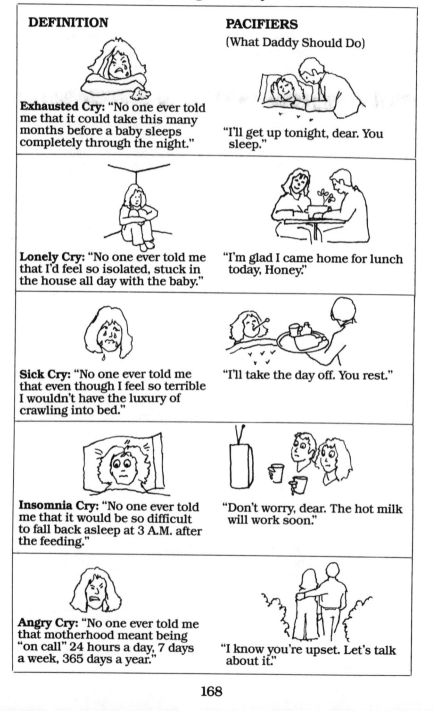

DEFINITION

Exhausted Cry: "No one ever told me that it could take this many months before a baby sleeps completely through the night."

PACIFIERS
(What Daddy Should Do)

"I'll get up tonight, dear. You sleep."

Lonely Cry: "No one ever told me that I'd feel so isolated, stuck in the house all day with the baby."

"I'm glad I came home for lunch today, Honey."

Sick Cry: "No one ever told me that even though I feel so terrible I wouldn't have the luxury of crawling into bed."

"I'll take the day off. You rest."

Insomnia Cry: "No one ever told me that it would be so difficult to fall back asleep at 3 A.M. after the feeding."

"Don't worry, dear. The hot milk will work soon."

Angry Cry: "No one ever told me that motherhood meant being "on call" 24 hours a day, 7 days a week, 365 days a year."

"I know you're upset. Let's talk about it."

Pick-Me-Ups for Mommy

When Mommy's suffering from guilt, anxieties ... and fears, she needs to lift her spirits with some good old-fashioned "spoiling". Here's a guide to special "pick-me-ups" just for Mommy.

Strawberry Stereo Slush

(Put on earphones, sip and listen while baby's napping.)

    1 cup skim milk
    1 cup fresh sliced strawberries
    3–4 ice cubes
    1 tsp. vanilla extract
    1 tsp. strawberry extract (opt.)
    Artificial sweetener (to taste)

Place all ingredients in blender and blend for 1 minute on high, pulsing on and off. Yield: 2 servings.

Calories: 70 cal. per serving

Peach Park Parfait

(Drink while cleaning sand and gravel out of baby's ears and toes, while making a list of everything you left behind at the park.)

    1/2 cup vanilla ice cream
    1/2 cup 2% milk
    1 cup fresh sliced peaches
    1 tsp. vanilla extract
    4 ice cubes

Place all ingredients in blender and blend for 1 minute on high, pulsing on and off. Yield: 2 servings.

Calories: 133 cal. per serving

Minty Mall Shimmer

(Perfect pick-me-up for afternoon out with Georgie.)

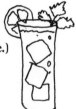

    1 tall glass iced tea
    1 slice lemon
    3 sprigs fresh mint
    Artificial sweetener (to taste)

Place in tall glass.

Calories: On the house

Rush Hour Refresher

(Enjoy ten minutes after you return home and before you start the dinner routine.)

    6 oz. cranberry juice
    1/4 cup orange juice
    1/2 cup ice chips
    1 tsp. lemon juice

Place all ingredients in tall glass and stir. Yield: 1 serving.

Calories: 166 cal. per serving

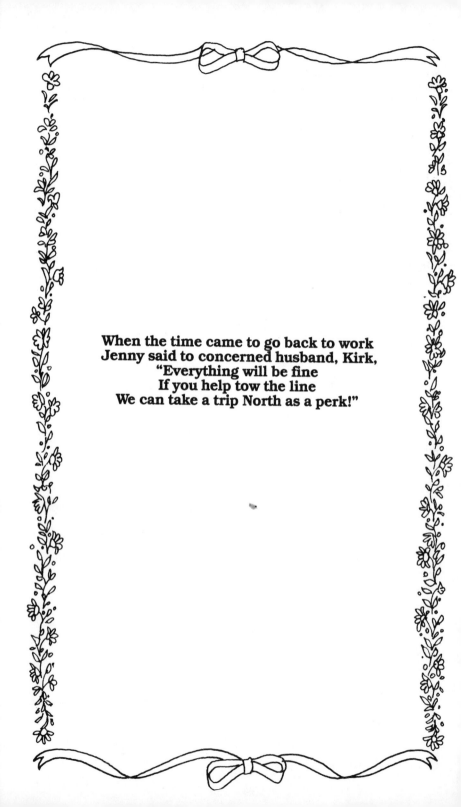

When the time came to go back to work
Jenny said to concerned husband, Kirk,
"Everything will be fine
If you help tow the line
We can take a trip North as a perk!"

Maternity Leave Expired

Returning to the Work at Hand

TCOM ADVISORS

Dear TCOM,

I'm at the crossroads of my life and am facing a dilemma. I'm a 31 year old career woman with an adorable four month old daughter. I've been happily married for nine years and have pursued a successful advertising career during that time.

Now, I'm ready to turn in my briefcase for a diaper bag ... permanently. I'm fortunate that my husband makes a nice living and I don't need to work, but I'm embarrassed to admit to others that I've chosen to stay at home.

I dread Saturday night cocktail parties because someone always asks, "And, what do you do?" I can't bear to reply, "I'm just a housewife!", for fear they'll think I'm boring.

Help! I can't keep ducking into the bathroom to avoid this question much longer.

Sincerely,

Stuck in the Can in Kansas

Dear C.K.:

Returning to work is a personal decision and you sound comfortable with your choice, though only in the confines of your own home. Our advice is to get off other people's potties and plunge into the needs of yourself and your family.

The Work Force
(Taking a Furlough vs. Reenlisting)

Mommies of the 80's are lucky. They have the capability and the childcare facilities available to combine both career and family, and the freedom of choice to trade in the **Wall Street Journal** for spending the rest of their days at home reading **Family Circle**.

However, it is sometimes difficult for Mommy to develop the confidence to handle public opinion about how she spends her days: "Don't you get bored just playing with the baby all day long?"; "Doesn't it bother you that someone else is raising your child ten hours a day?"

Whether or not Mommy returns to work, as a result of a financial need or a desire to pursue a personal goal, she must feel comfortable with the decision she makes. It's only when Mommy is confident with her choice of lifestyle that she won't stew about what her neighbor, her mother-in-law, or her hairdresser thinks.

Workman's Compensation
(The Ramifications of a Second Income)

Mommy must reexamine the bottom line before returning to work, since childcare expenses will now alter the end result. A second income of $20,000/year, which may have afforded the luxury of a trip up north, may now only sustain a trip to the grocery store. Often what Mommy thinks she will be earning isn't always what she will bank.

Read through this example prepared by a Certified Public Accountant (CPA) and discover what happens to Mommy on payday.

Analysis of Mommy's Disposable Income
Examining Mommy's Paycheck
Judith R. Trepeck, C.P.A.
GREY, TREPECK & COHEN, P.C.

When examining what's really left from Mommy's salary, she has to keep a few things in mind. Various taxes must be paid: federal income tax, state and city income taxes where applicable, and social security taxes. Mommy must also consider the family's tax bracket. Federal income taxes are graduated and she will be putting her income on top of what's already there.

Assumptions:
- Married
- 39% tax bracket, i.e., $35,200–$45,800 taxable income; family's taxable income before Mommy's taxable income is $26,800.
- Second income of $20,000

Gross Income	$20,000
Marriage penalty relief 1982–5% 1983–10%	1,000
Mommy's Taxable Income	19,000
Federal Income Tax (effective rate is 33.9%)	6,782
Michigan Income Tax 1982–5.1% 1983–6.35%	1,020
Social Security Tax (6.7%)	1,340
Total Taxes	9,142

Money available before Child Care Expense	10,858

Child Care Expense*
  One child for 50 weeks @ $60 per week—
  Net of $480 Child Care Credit in 1982   2,520

Disposable Income
  What's left before Mommy deducts her
  undeterminable costs $ 8,338

Mommy's Undeterminable Costs

1. Meals

2. Clothing

3. Personal Care

4. Auto Expense-commuting to and from work; additional maintenance, additional insurance

5. Physical and Psychological wear and tear

6. Life Insurance

7. Disability Insurance

8. Housekeeping and Maintenance Expenses

9. Out-of-Pocket, Unreimbursed Business Expenses

10. Education Expenses, Unreimbursed

*This may be low, especially if Mommy has private child care in her home.

The Work Week: The Part-time Option
("Does less equal more?")

Working part-time presents Mommy with the "best of both worlds". When it is available, do consider its benefits:

- It allows Mommy to achieve personal and financial goals without feeling the guilt of leaving the children for a long period of time.

- It relieves Mommy's anxiety and pressure by reducing her work load, thus freeing up another 20 hours per week of Mommy's time for herself and her family.

- It provides Mommy with a financial option that may be more advantageous than working full-time, due to taxes and childcare.

 **The Job-Sharing Option**

When part-time work isn't available, some Mommies create their own by job-sharing. Two Mommies, who are capable of performing the same job, agree to split the hours, the responsibility, and the salary of one full-time position.

(**TCOM Hint:** Be sure you get your boss' permission before "going halfsies".)

Easiest Times for Mommy to Go Back to Work	Worst Times for Mommy to Go Back to Work
1. When the baby is still an infant (adapts easily to Mommy working).	1. When the children are in the preschool stage, before age five, and are readily upset by changes in Mommy's routine.
2. When the children are six and older (in elementary school) and do not need Mommy's constant attention.	2. When the children are in early adolescence – the struggle for independence vs. the need for strong parent involvement.

According to Jean Curtis, **Working Mothers**

Working It Out
(Re-evaluating "Rolls")

Mommy's decision to go back to work requires Daddy's support because he, too, must be willing to take on a second job. Mommy and Daddy need to set priorities, divide responsibilities, and determine how they will function on a daily basis to get dinner on the table and clean clothes in the bureau drawers.

Two bread "winners" necessitates two bread "bakers". Since working Mommies need well-defined "rolls", here's an assortment from which Mommy can choose.

TCOM Presents: The Baker's Special

 The Jelly Roll: The nervous Mommy. She's not sure she can handle the responsibility of working *and* the demands of her new family.

 The Crescent Roll: The flaky Mommy. She has good intentions, loves the thought of returning to work, but can't find one idea to stick to for more than 24 hours.

 The Sandwich Roll: The squeezed Mommy. She's caught between the desire to stay at home and the financial need to return to work.

 The Day Old Roll: The "I-tried-it-and-I-didn't-like-it" Mommy. She returns to work for one day after her maternity leave is up and quits.

 The Hard Roll: The tough Mommy. When childless, she lacked compassion for new Mommies returning to work. But now that she's had a child of her own, she's the first one in the parking lot when the whistle blows.

 The Sweet Roll: The content Mommy. She can juggle the demands of her job and her home and do it all well.

 The Dinner Roll: The old-fashioned Mommy. She happily assumes all of the household responsibilities (she'd never think of asking for Daddy's help) and works, too.

The Cloverleaf Roll: The lucky Mommy. She's found a job that allows her the flexibility to work at home and can "have her cake and eat it, too."

TCOM Survey Results

"Did you return to work?"	Average length of maternity leave:	Average hours per week at work:
Yes 42% No 58%	2 months	26 hours

The Workplace
(Working Inside the Home vs. Working Outside of the Home)

Working Inside the Home

1. **Old eagle eye:** Mommy can watch over the household.

   Mommy may not like what she sees or may spend the entire day watching.

2. **Reduced expenses:** Mommy can save money on office, food, transportation, childcare, and clothing.

   Mommy may also reduce productivity unless she is very disciplined.

3. **Kitchen privileges:** Mommy can be close to the kitchen for plenty of coffee and food.

   Beware: Mommy may be abusing the privileges if she is the third stop on the Hostess man's delivery route.

4. **Flextime:** Mommy can schedule her hours so she's not "rained out" by sick children, bad weather, or car trouble.

   Mommy may not have the opportunity or the luxury to "escape" or be snowed in, since her work is always there.

5. **Proximity:** Mommy can be close to the children in case they need her.

   Unfortunately, this may encompass everything from needing a "boo boo" kissed to needing a "Candyland" partner.

Working Outside of the Home

1. **Grown-up stimulation:** Mommy can interact with adults.

   Mommy may also have the companion pressures of office gossip and politics.

2. **Work commitment:** Mommy must be at a specific place at a specific time to perform a specific task.

   Mommy may lose flexibility, since she is dependent upon specific schedules and reliable childcare.

3. **Concentration:** Mommy can focus on work in a work atmosphere without the distraction of home.

   Beware: Mommy may spend time focusing on what's going on at home, rather than on work.

4. **Dressing up:** Mommy must consider her appearance, leaving her blue jeans and robe behind.

   Mommy may need to spend money to "dress for success".

5. **Steady income:** Mommy can receive a regular paycheck and some form of benefits.

   Mommy may be at the mercy of someone else's control.

Workable Childcare

Some Mommies prefer to hire help to come into the home, while others feel more comfortable placing their child in a reputable childcare facility. Regardless, Mommy cannot return to work without a responsible childcare plan. Investigate, interview, and sample (See "Help/Help!"). Here are some important factors to consider:

- Certified by the state

- Philosophy of program: physical *and* mental space.

- Routine: rest, meals, snacks, play at regularly planned times for consistency.

- Sick policy: strict rules forbidding attendance when ill.

- Parental involvement: regular progress reports and active parent participation.

- Ratio of teacher to child

- Environment: clean, well-stocked materials and equipment.

- Caregivers: warm, loving, affectionate, articulate, patient, creative, and secure.

- Health and safety precautions.

- Cost.

Workable Solutions
Relieving Guilt

Mommy's often been told that it is the quality of the time she spends with her children, not the quantity, that is important.

However true this statement may be, it doesn't quite comfort Mommy when she feels guilty about her decision to return to work. Intellectually, Mommy thinks everything will be okay, but emotionally, she's convinced that her adorable five month old Jason will grow up to be Attila the Hun due to her absence from nine to five.

Here are six **TCOM** steps designed to relieve Mommy's pangs of guilt by ensuring that the time Mommy does spend with her baby is "quality time".

Step 1: Spend one hour everyday with the baby ... exclusively.

"Oh, I'm so excited, I just love my hour alone with Mommy!"

"I wish Mommy would turn off the TV and play with me."

Step 2: Establish a bedtime routine ... and follow it every night.

"After my double diaper I know Mommy's going to hold me and sing her lullaby and ..."

"Wait a minute ... rocking me now? I'm not in my sleepers yet! I'm not diapered ... help!"

Step 3: Plan family time together ... every weekend.

"Goody! Mommy's getting out the bike. I just love Saturday afternoon bike rides."

"Mrs. Henderson, again ... I wish Mommy would spend time with me. I'd love to go shopping with her ..."

Step 4: Select a caregiver ... your child adores.

"Oh boy, I just love Mrs. Mackie ... I can't wait to see her ... I hope she reads me **Pat the Bunny.**"

"Boy, I wish Mommy would find someone I liked to stay with me me when she has to leave."

Step 5: Share special times with the baby ... including important milestones.

"Mommy's so special ... she took the day off just so she could take me to get my first pair of shoes."

"Humph. My first pair of shoes ... I wish Mommy would stop trying on sneakers and help me decide between the high tops or the low tops."

Step 6: Include the baby in the daily routine ... from the start.

"I just love going from room to room, keeping Mommy company while she does her chores."

"I wish Mommy wouldn't stick me me in the playpen, while she vacuums. I love being close to her."

Get Me To The Office On Time
Don't even think you can get to the office on time if ...

You push the snooze control more than three times.

You took your week's supply of Ex-lax last night.

You forgot to fill the car with gas.

You take a shower with Daddy.

You are looking for your wallet at 7:15, your keys at 7:30 and your glasses at 7:45.

You haven't the foggiest idea what you're going to wear.

You stop to sew name tags in all of Bobby's clothes before dropping him at the daycare center.

You take time to pump iron, iron your blazer, and iron out your problems.

You don't have a regular, well-planned routine.

Mommy's Work Bag

Before   **After**

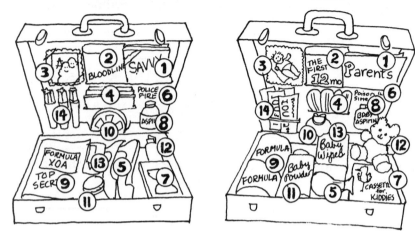

KEY

1. Coffee break reading
2. Lunchtime reading
3. Snapshot
4. Assorted pads
5. Pumps
6. Emergency numbers
7. Cassettes
8. First aid
9. Formula
10. Software
11. Powder
12. Security
13. Wipes
14. Markers

Meet the 1980's Work Horse

TGIF ... you're pooped, but you're proud. You've done a great job of keeping yourself and your family together through another work week. You're looking forward to a quiet, undemanding weekend to refuel.

But your mother-in-law has other ideas. She simply must serve *your* 7 hour, 11 layer jello mold at tomorrow's bridge game.

For mothers-in-law, Daddies, and other well-meaning friends who send Mommy reaching for her fluted mold and bing cherries, **TCOM** presents these new interpretations of "Mommy's state of exhaustion".

"But, Mom, you don't understand, I'm so exhaused that ..."

1. I'm actually considering serving Rice Krispies with bananas and cream for Uncle Sidney's 50th Birthday party.

2. I've worn my navy suit with my white turtleneck for the past 11 days and what's worse, I intend to wear it for at least 11 more.

3. I've lost my hair, my sense of humor, my way to the ladies' room ... and I've only been back at work for three days.

4. I repeat myself six times before I think someone hears me.

5. I repeat myself six times before I think someone hears me.

6. I've got that "I've-been-cramming-for-finals-look" and I've been out of school for 15 years.

7. Stanley's hired a lifeguard to watch over me while I take my bath.

8. My "bags" are so well packed that Samsonite wants my advice on their new fall line.

9. My body's given in ... I'm taking Tetracycline every six hours, Excedrin every four hours, and requests for all my worldly possessions.

10. When Stanley told me he was bringing "The Colonel" home for dinner, I pulled out the crystal and made Beef Stroganoff.

Millie planned her reunion with Pete
So that baby John wouldn't compete,
An evening of dancing
And quiet romancing
Made their first night together complete.

Sex

The "R" Rated Chapter

Waiting for the Light to Turn Green

According to the **Taking Care Of Mommy** Survey, 98% of the Mommies gave the following response when asked "Did you have any tips for feeling sexy during the rather unsexy time of postpartum?"

"I didn't!"

Getting the Green Light

Before you draw the bubble-bath-for-two and put the champagne on ice, Mommy's first order of business is to schedule her six week checkup with her obstetrician. Here's the standard procedure she can expect:

- Internal examination to make sure her stitches have healed properly and that everything is back to normal.

- Pap smear.

- Breast examination.

- Weight—usually followed by a frown, clearing of throat and/or lecture.

- Discussion of menstrual cycle (returns usually 4-14 weeks after childbirth).

- Contraceptives—discussed and prescribed.

- Discussion of sexual relations, hemorrhoids, vitamins and iron.

- (optional) Mommy offers her doctor $20 *not* to mention to Daddy that it's okay to have sex.

Contraception

Since a repeat pregnancy is the **last** thing a new Mommy needs, here is a postpartum refresher course in contraception.

Method	Effectiveness (%)
Abstinence	100
Sterilization	99.7-99.8
Birth Control Pill	99.8-99.9
IUD	97-98
Diaphragm (and Spermicide)	95-97
Vaginal Sponge	95
Condom and Foam	95-97
Condom	90-92
Foam, Jellies, Vaginal Suppositories (Spermicides)	90
Coitus Interruptus	85
Rhythm (Sympto-Thermal Method)	82

(**TCOM Hint:** Breast feeding is not a form of birth control. You can get pregnant the first time you ovulate before you begin to menstruate again.)

After the Light Turns Green

Many women are not interested in resuming sexual relations at this time ... they are giving so much of themselves to the baby because his needs are so enormous during the first three months, they have nothing left over for the husband ...

Motherhood, Your First 12 Months
Deborah Insel

There is stress and strain in even the best relationship because of exhaustion and coping with so many changes. Many Mommies are anxious to resume the closeness, but fearful of the encounter: "Will it hurt?" (Yes), "Where will I find the energy?" (Halfway between the kitchen and the bedroom), "What if the baby starts screaming in the middle?" (So, what if the baby starts screaming in the middle?), "Lack of lubrication?, Chance of infection?" (A pre-lubricated condom will solve both problems).

To minimize the anxiety of Mommy's "first reunion" with Daddy, (and to offer a few hints) **TCOM** presents, "The Story of Bob and Martha".

How To Make Love Successfully
The First Time After Childbirth

Martha's Mom arrives to spend the night.	Bob and Martha leave.	Bob and Martha go out for an intimate dinner.
Bob and Martha order dinner.	Bob talks about his promotion.	Martha talks about freelancing.
Bob requests their wedding song.	Bob whispers "sweet nothings" in Martha's ear.	Martha whispers in Bob's ear.
Bob and Martha make a B-line for the door.	Bob and Martha check into the motel.	Bob chills the wine.
*Martha slips on her negligee.	Bob turns off the lights, turns on the music...and Martha.	Bob and Martha smile. They've still got it.

*Martha should also slip on some K-Y Jelly; Bob should slip on a condom to prevent infection (check with your doctor).

10 Best Places to Make Love to Escape From The Baby

1. In the garage ... under the car.

2. In the front hall closet ... under Daddy's trenchcoat.

3. In the tree house ... "In front of the squirrels?"

4. In the basement ... behind the furnace.

5. On the balcony ... next to the pink geraniums.

6. On the kitchen floor ... waiting for the formula to be sterilized.

7. Under the bed ... between sneezes and wheezes.

8. In the bathtub ... with the shower running.

9. In the play pen ... between the activity center and the hanging gym.

10. In the library ... between Spock and Brazelton.

When the Light Never Turns Green

Some Mommies wait four weeks after delivery before resuming sexual relations. Some wait six weeks. And some wait eight.

For those of you who are still waiting, we offer the following:

The Joy of Abstinence
The Joy of Never Having to Worry About ...

- When your last period was due

- If your old diaphragm fits

- Being interrupted by the baby

- Is the foam fresh?

- Eating onions and garlic

- The phone ringing

- Your neighborhood pharmacist winking at you

How Mommy and Daddy Can Have the Best-Relationship-in-the-Whole-Wide-World

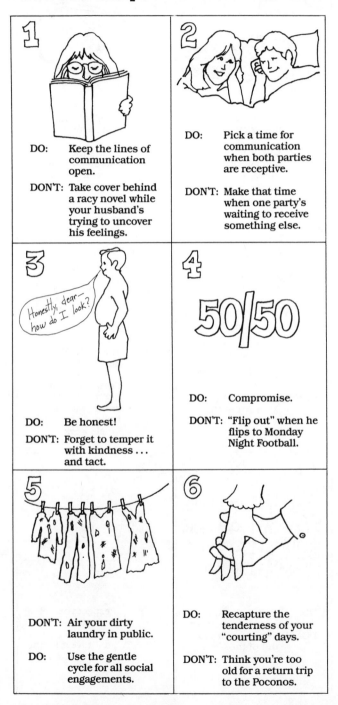

1

DO: Keep the lines of communication open.

DON'T: Take cover behind a racy novel while your husband's trying to uncover his feelings.

2

DO: Pick a time for communication when both parties are receptive.

DON'T: Make that time when one party's waiting to receive something else.

3

Honestly, dear— how do I look?

DO: Be honest!

DON'T: Forget to temper it with kindness ... and tact.

4

50/50

DO: Compromise.

DON'T: "Flip out" when he flips to Monday Night Football.

5

DON'T: Air your dirty laundry in public.

DO: Use the gentle cycle for all social engagements.

6

DO: Recapture the tenderness of your "courting" days.

DON'T: Think you're too old for a return trip to the Poconos.

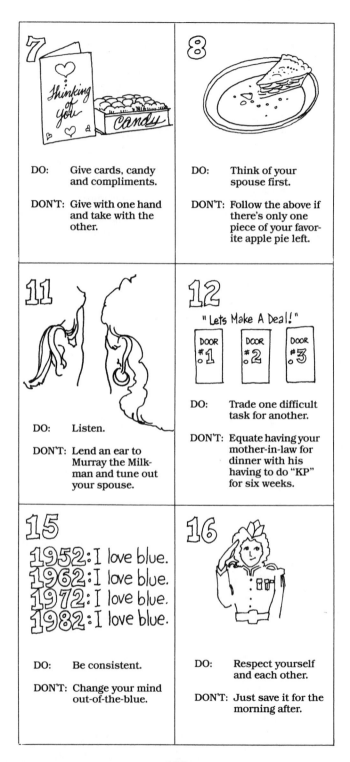

7

DO: Give cards, candy and compliments.

DON'T: Give with one hand and take with the other.

8

DO: Think of your spouse first.

DON'T: Follow the above if there's only one piece of your favorite apple pie left.

11

DO: Listen.

DON'T: Lend an ear to Murray the Milkman and tune out your spouse.

12

"Let's Make A Deal!"

DOOR #1 DOOR #2 DOOR #3

DO: Trade one difficult task for another.

DON'T: Equate having your mother-in-law for dinner with his having to do "KP" for six weeks.

15

1952: I love blue.
1962: I love blue.
1972: I love blue.
1982: I love blue.

DO: Be consistent.

DON'T: Change your mind out-of-the-blue.

16

DO: Respect yourself and each other.

DON'T: Just save it for the morning after.

9

DON'T: Make love unless you both want to.

DO: Give it your best shot ... bring *him* two aspirin and model your sexy new nightgown.

10

DO: Check your vocabulary and gestures; soften your words and touch.

DON'T: Call each other anything that's not in *Webster's.*

13

DO: Establish strong support systems for each other.

DON'T: Get unhooked when things get tight.

14

DON'T: Forget to save time for fun and frivolity.

DO: "It" with your spouse.

17

DO: Make an effort to do one thing every day for your spouse.

DON'T: Wrap it up with strings attached.

18

DO: Thank your lucky stars.

DON'T: Forget the beautiful baby in the nursery.

189

From the start it was Marilyn's aim
To get Tom in the parenting game,
All his efforts were praised
And his confidence raised
Now "quick changes" are his claim to fame.

Coparenting

Making Room for Daddy

Daddies' Waiting Room
(Yesterday)

Daddies' Waiting Room
(Today)

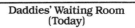

Once upon a time when Daddy was expecting his first child, he made sure he had comfortable shoes, a big box of cigars, and the Sunday edition of the **Times**. He was prepared to pace until the spring thaw or the birth of his child.

Then one day, as the 419,478,542 Daddy (Harold Steinberger) was being ushered to the waiting room he threw himself on the corridor floor and exclaimed, "Wait! I've got the stop watch, the rolling pin, and the breathing down pat. Let this Daddy go ... in with Mommy!"

Suddenly, the labor room doors flew open. And so did delivery. And recovery. And the nursery. And the kitchen. And the laundry room...

And in walked Harold. Soon to be followed by John and Frank and Harvey and Steve and ... marking the beginning of a new era of involvement for Daddy.

Suddenly Daddies everywhere are ready and willing. Now it's Mommy's responsibility to make them able. Coparenting is a four-handed job. Since Mommy's needs vary, the degrees of Daddy's involvement differ as well. The objective of coparenting is to find a *consistent framework* that meets the needs of both Mommy and Daddy.

Involving Daddy on the Ground Floor

Daddy will be a more cooperative partner when he's included from the start and made to feel that his opinions count. (Don't ask what he thinks about disposable diapers **after** you've just signed a two year contract with Dydee Service.)

Inspire Daddy to roll up his sleeves by encouraging discussion of the following:

1. **Negotiate Tasks** "Divvy up" the responsibilities—Mommy and Daddy should *both* make choices about the jobs they want to do. (Mommy should not routinely assign chores to Daddy and expect them to be carried out!)

2. **Inform Daddy** Share the baby's development with Daddy on a *daily* basis; Daddy is just as excited as Mommy is about all of the baby's "firsts". (Mommy should not conceal the baby's progress!)

3. **Discuss All Decisions** Mommy and Daddy should develop a child rearing philosophy *together.* (Mommy should not draw up ground rules alone!)

4. **Plan Family Time** Set aside free time for activities which *both* Mommy and Daddy find fun and exciting. (Mommy should not steal Daddy's proxy. Both Mommy and Daddy get an equal vote. In case of a tie, flip a coin!)

5. **Share Knowledge** Update Daddy on new babycare skills and information, including tips from Mommy's best friend. (Mommy should not hold a superior attitude about child-care ... she was a novice at one time, too!)

Harold's Father Takes a Cruise...Permanently!

Mommies of today are further ahead than Mommies of yester-year due to the willingness of today's Daddies to assume a more involved role. The next time you think Daddy has "missed the boat", reread case study #D-683.

Case Study #D-683: The Steinbergers

Circa 1950   Circa 1980

	Harold's Father	Harold
"It's bathtime"	"Bye-bye, Honey. Have fun with Mommy."	"C'mon, Sweetheart. Let's go find Rubber Duckie. I'm the bubble man tonight."
"It's dinnertime"	"Boy, am I starved!"	"C'mon, Pumpkin. Into the Snugli while Daddy flips his famous burgers."
"It's bedtime"	"Nite-nite, Honey."	"C'mon, Angel. Daddy's going to rock you. Lulla-bye and goodnight..."
"It's naptime"	"Nite-nite, Honey."	"C'mon, Sweetie. Let's change your diaper and wind the mobile."
"It's playtime"	"Bye-bye, Honey. Have fun with Mommy."	"C'mon, Peanut. Let's find your favorite rattle and Peek-A-Boo Bunny."
"It's clean up time"	"I'll go upstairs and get out of your way."	"C'mon, Babydoll. You stay right here while Daddy puts all these toys away."
"It's laundry time"	"I need my blue and white striped shirt ironed by tomorrow, Honey."	"C'mon, Muffin. Help Daddy sort the laundry while the machine's filling up."

You're Welcome
The "Honey, Look-What-I-Did-For-You" Syndrome

Most Daddies have been conditioned since birth that caring for the house and the baby are Mommy's domain. However, in recent years, many Daddies have also been conditioned to pitch in and lend Mommy a helping hand. This has created a "strange" phenomenon.

As helpful as Daddy may be, from changing the diapers to changing the sheets, he always seems to be giving Mommy a look of "You're welcome!", since he feels he's just completed "her" chores.

Therefore, even though Daddy will readily assist Mommy (often without being asked), beware of this "knowing nod". It will follow a completed task. And it will mean, "You owe me one."

TCOM Survey Results: Does your husband help with the baby:

61% replied, "Often"
26% replied, "Sometimes"
13% replied, "Never"

When asked what tasks Daddy helps with:

80% babysit
79% feed baby
64% bedtime
59% change diapers
49% make formula
36% bathe baby
18% night feedings

Mommy's Obedience School

Daddy needs the confidence and security that can only come from Mommy's praise and guidance. Too often, though, Mommy's possessiveness of the baby causes her to condescend, instead of coddle, Daddy and his childcare attempts.

Criticism can thwart a potentially helpful Daddy's efforts more quickly than anything. And so can harsh words. Beware of "barking" orders at Daddy. Take the time to speak to him in a reasonable tone.

10 Words or Phrases Mommy Should NEVER Use When Speaking to Daddy

1. Fetch!
2. Sit!
3. Jump!
4. Roll over!
5. Beg
6. Heel!
7. Down, boy!
8. Here, boy!
9. Good, boy!
10. Not tonight, boy!

Taking Care of Mommy Board of Trade
(Quid Pro Quo)

Dividing up chores is a matter of personal preference. While one parent will do almost anything to avoid laundry, another would eagerly wash day and night if it meant never having to change another dirty diaper. Therefore, to promote fair trade between Mommy and Daddy, *both* must first agree on what "quid" equals what "quo".

The TCOM Board of Trade presents examples of an equitable exchange. (Allowing Harold to watch the NFL Playoffs, distraction free, is not worthy of assigning him "K.P." until Christmas—unless the game goes into overtime!)

Review the trade-offs presented here, then take the time to work out your own ... together.

No. 1: The Diaper Change

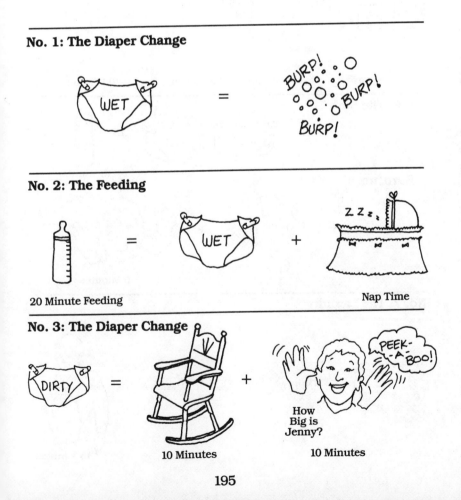

No. 2: The Feeding

20 Minute Feeding

Nap Time

No. 3: The Diaper Change

10 Minutes

How Big is Jenny?

10 Minutes

No. 4: Dressing

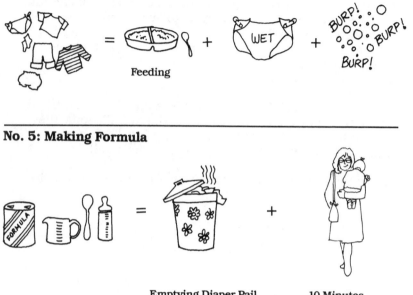

Feeding

No. 5: Making Formula

Emptying Diaper Pail   10 Minutes

No. 6: The Bath

10 Minutes

Bathtub

5 Minutes

No. 7: The Laundry

15 Minutes

No. 8: Cleaning Nursery

Patty Cake
Patty Cake

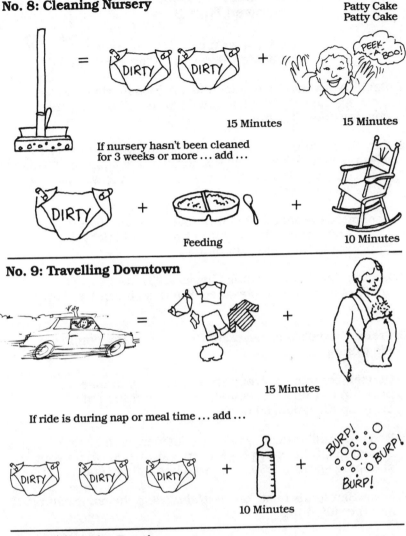

= DIRTY DIRTY + PEEK-A-BOO!

15 Minutes   15 Minutes

If nursery hasn't been cleaned
for 3 weeks or more ... add ...

DIRTY + Feeding + 10 Minutes

No. 9: Travelling Downtown

= 15 Minutes +

If ride is during nap or meal time ... add ...

DIRTY + DIRTY + DIRTY + 10 Minutes + BURP! BURP! BURP!

No. 10: Nite-Nite Routine

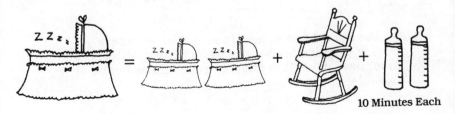

ZZz = ZZz + ZZz + 10 Minutes Each

10 Minutes

Father Knows Best . . . Because Mommy Showed Him How!

Ten Easy Steps to Turning Harold into the World's Greatest Daddy

1. **Decide** with Harold which childcare jobs he wants to do. (Leaving the baby at his mother's house while he goes bowling doesn't count.)

2. **Explain** to Harold (without being bossy) what's involved with the task he's chosen. (Avoid these declarations: "This is the only way to hold the baby ... This is the way you better feed the baby.")

3. **Acclimate** Harold into his new role ... slowly. (Don't run off for eight hours the very first time Harold babysits, returning to find him catatonic.)

4. **Inspire** Harold to try things his way. ("Harold, I can't get Sara to eat her applesauce. You're so inventive, would you try?"

5. **Praise** Harold's successes. (If there aren't any, commend his willingness to try.)

   (Remember to be appropriate. Give enough praise to bring up Harold's self-confidence, but not too much to bring up his chicken pot pie.)

6. **Boost** Harold's success rate by considering the baby's schedule. (If the baby poops every day at 1:00, go on your shopping spree at 1:30, so Harold has a clean start.)

7. **Show** Harold his mistakes *tactfully*. (Skip the name calling, and the ridiculing.)

   ("Thanks, Harold, for putting the baby in a clean sleeper. Gee, isn't it funny, I once forgot to put a diaper on the baby, too.")

8. **Remind** Harold how long it took you to become a "pro" and that practice really does make perfect. ("Gee, Harold, I must have made this crib a hundred times before I got it right.")

9. **Encourage** Harold to master the small tasks before moving on to the larger ones. ("Gee, Harold, I think it's wonderful that you want to take the baby on your hunting trip. But, maybe you should start with a few hours of baby-sitting first?")

10. **Hug** Harold often and tell him how important he is. ("Harold, you're the world's greatest Daddy!")

Formula for the "Unforgettable" Daddy

You now have the **TCOM** basics for "making room for Daddy". Add Mommy's special brand of warmth to Daddy's innate goodness and success will be imminent.

While you are turning your spouse into an involved Daddy, remember: no one can ever be perfect. So, strive for a balance that satisfies both Mommy's and Daddy's needs and you'll have a winning combination for coparenting.

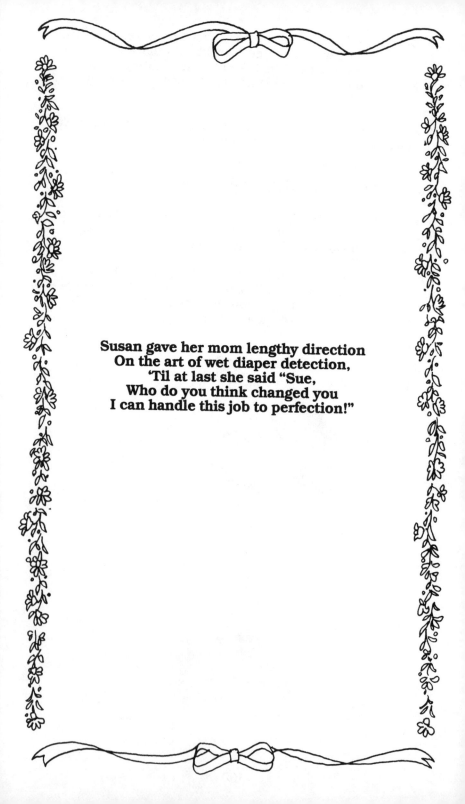

Susan gave her mom lengthy direction
On the art of wet diaper detection,
'Til at last she said "Sue,
Who do you think changed you
I can handle this job to perfection!"

Grandmothers
Mommy's Grandest Helpers

G is for Grandmother through the ages

While the grandmas of today have traded in babushka and housecoat for windblown hair and jeans, their grandmotherly love remains constant. Indeed, grandparents-to-be are almost as excited as parents-to-be, especially if this is going to be their first grandchild.

Though grandmother's love has never waned through the ages, time commitments and priorities have shifted due to changing lifestyles. The "me" generation philosophy of the 1980's has spilled into the current generation of grandmothers. No longer content to just bake cookies and clean house, today's world has given grandmothers the opportunity to add greater dimension to their lives.

While grandma anxiously looks forward to special moments with her grandchild, she must now schedule those moments in between her other engagements, like working, working out, and being worked over (nails and hair). And due to increased mobility, it is not uncommon for grandma to be gone several months out of the year. Thus, there is less time available for Mommy, Daddy, and baby to spend with grandma. Here's a guide to making the most of the precious time you all have to share.

R is for the respect you'd like so much

Parents become more involved with both sets of grandparents after the birth of the first child. Depending upon the preexisting relationships, this can be a wonderful or a disastrous experience.

Some couples are still harboring conflicts that centered around the wedding ("I still can't believe your mother wouldn't pose with my mother for the family picture!"), others have varied standards and values ("I'm sorry if it hurts your mother's feelings, my child is not wearing a fur bunting!"), while others enjoy a harmonious relationship ("Isn't it sweet that my mom's taking the first week and your mom's taking the second week after the baby's born!").

Many times grandparents look forward to the birth of their first grandchild so they can regain some of the control they lost when their children were married. (They hope that the presence of the baby will provide them with the opportunity to assume a stronger role.)

Many grandparents have difficulty accepting that their "children" are now "parents", independent and responsible for another human being. Hence, the importance of Mommy and Daddy presenting a "united front".

Four of the Reasons Ozzie and Harriet Never Fought
(about grandmothers ... or anything else!)

1. They agreed to present a united front. They never allowed grandma to "pit" Harriet against Ozzie to gain control.

2. They openly discussed any problems their parents presented. ("Harriet, this is the fourth time this week we've had your mother for dinner. We need to talk!")

3. They recognized that parents can forgive "words" with their own children more easily than "words" with their "in-law" children. (Ozzie always worked it out with his mom and Harriet always worked it out with hers!)

4. They agreed over what, and what not, to make a fuss about. ("Ozzie dear, don't you think you were a little hard on your mother because she bought the kids a pack of gum?" "But, Harriet, she also packed them full of gumdrops, taffy, jelly beans, and soda pop!")

A shows Gram's appreciated by Mommy

The birth of your child triggers many emotions and feelings about your relationship with your own mother. Mommies usually develop a new closeness to their mothers, or at least a new appreciation of what motherhood is all about.

At this time of transition, you may be open to an understanding of the long, long chain of mother-daughter feelings and ties based upon being the female child of a female. This understanding can have a profound healing effect on your relationship with your mother, freeing your positive feelings about her and allowing your own unique motherhood to take shape.

> Lyn DelliQuadri, MSW, and Kati Breckenridge, PhD,
> **Mothercare**

You can now understand your own mother's words of yesteryear, "One day when you have a child of your own, you'll understand just how Mommy feels".

Mommy appreciates Grandma and shows it by . . .

1. Sending grandma roses on Mommy's birthday as a "Thanks for giving me life" gift.

2. Hiring a babysitter and taking grandma to lunch.

3. Including grandma in your family portrait (have her stand on the far left, so you can snip her off when you send your mother-in-law a copy).

4. Inviting grandma over and cooking her favorite meal.

5. Dressing all of your children in "My Grandma's the Best!" T-shirts.

N is for noting new roles, new names, and such

This is a perplexing time for many Mommies, who find themselves torn between the need for guidance and the need for independence. Mommy wants the support, but she doesn't want to be controlled.

While it's "normal" for your mother to help you during the first few weeks after the baby, if you want her to view you as an independent, self-sufficient mother you must have her move out before the child's high school graduation.

Consistency is vital. You can't call your mother and sob everyday for three weeks only to get angry when she offers her advice unsolicited the following week.

Finally, be patient. The transition from "daughter" to "mother" is a slow one. You will always be your "mommy's little girl", but in time you will get her to respect you as a "Mommy" as well.

> For many women, the struggle for independence and an identity distinct from their mother's makes it difficult to ask for emotional support and help during childbearing. But, you should be assured that you are not regressing if you need your mother at the time you bear your own child.
>
> Lyn DelliQuadri, MSW and Kati Breckenridge, PhD, **Mothercare**

TCOM Survey Results: "What was the nicest thing grandma did and what was the worst thing she did concerning the baby?"

Nicest Thing:

49% Babysit
32% Help with meals
19% Stay overnight
and help

Worst Thing:

42% Too much unsolicited
advice
38% Made Mommy feel
inadequate
20% Visited too often

---

is darling daughter's rules for grandma.

Mommy's Rules for Grandma

Guidelines for being the kind of grandma
Mommy will love having around

1. Please don't give us advice on raising children unless we ask for it.

2. Please don't interfere once we've made decisions or established routines and rules.

3. We will make mistakes, just like you did. Allow us that right. We will eventually learn and see the light.

4. If we do ask for specific advice, please direct your opinion to that one topic. This is not a license for giving advice across the board.

5. When you babysit, we would appreciate it if you would follow our rules, schedules, and guidelines as closely as possible. We do understand that you need to be softer and easier. Use common sense and your big hearts.

6. Be honest with us and about your feelings — tell us how you feel, but please don't tell us what to do!

7. Don't avoid confrontations by sweeping problems under the rug. We can have an open, warm relationship if we keep communicating.

8. Please give us the room to run our own lives, but stay close enough so we can share the special moments together.

Adapted from Dr. Fitzhugh Dodson, **How to Grandparent**

M is the many things she'll have on hand

Here's a guide to stocking grandma's house with all the things needed to make Mommy's life easier. The next time you go to grandma's, you can jump into the family Buick and leave the U-Haul behind.

Stocking Grandma's House

1. **The Pack-in-Three-Hours-and-You're-There Plan**

   When the only things Grandma provides are:

   | diapers (regular) | diapers (spit up) | *reams of plastic |
   | diapers (disposable) | | |

   *when you start packing call Grandma so she can begin covering the furniture!

2. **The Pack-in-Thirty-Minutes-and-You're-There Plan**

   When Grandma provides all of the above, plus:

feeding spoons	small assortment	a place to sleep
dishes	of baby food	the baby
bibs	wipes	a place to change
formula, bottles,	rattle	the baby
nipples		

3. The I-Was-in-the-Neighborhood-and-I-Thought-I'd-Drop-by Plan

When Grandma provides all of the above, plus:

the entire line of Gerber, Heinz, and Beechnut baby food.	Nanny, babysitter, clown, VHS of "Sesame Street"	½ dozen undershirts, ½ dozen socks
a changing table	Fisher-Price, Child Guidance, Ambi, and Hasbro toys	3 sleepers and 2 outfits
a crib, playpen, swing		

Turning Grandma into Mommy's Grandest Sitter

1. It's easier to babysit in the baby's home (the one exception is infancy, when the baby sleeps comfortably for long periods of time anywhere.)

2. Baby's more comfortable in his own environment, especially as he gets older. A child-proofed home is safer than a grandparent's haven of lifetime possessions.

3. Grandmas need time off, too, and should speak up when they need a break.

4. Make sure Grandma has the following information when Mommy leaves the house:

   a) child's doctor
   b) nearest poison control
   c) paramedics
   d) fire department
   e) police station

5. Always leave a number where Mommy can be reached, including itinerary if out of town. Mommy should call home as often as she needs to for everyone's sake.

Adapted from Dr. Fitzhugh Dodson, **How to Grandparent**

What Mommy says isn't always what grandma hears.

What Mommy Says	**What Grandma Hears**
"Mom ... please put Jenny down for a nap between 2:30 and 3:15. Thanks."	"Nap? Well, dear, she just didn't look tired to me and she just wouldn't go to sleep!"
"Mom ... can you please give the baby half a jar of applesauce and half a bowl of cereal for lunch — that's her favorite. Thanks."	"Lunch? Oh, she ate a wonderful lunch, dear ... half a jar of peaches, half a jar of pears, half a jar of peas, and a bottle of juice."
"Mom ... after the baby gets up from her nap, please let her play a little by herself. It's too much for you to play with her every minute. Thanks."	"Playtime? All she wanted me to do was hold her all morning long, dear. I didn't mind. I just loved it."
"Mom ... please change Jenny's diaper often and use a little vaseline. Thanks."	"Diapers? When was the last time I changed her diaper? Was I supposed to change her diaper ... Oh dear!"
"Mom ... when the baby gets up, please dress her in the little pink overalls and matching shirt, shoes, and socks I left on the changing table. Thanks."	"Clothes? Pink overalls? I found this adorable yellow outfit in the closet. It's much cuter, dear."

O is for the Old Wives Tales she'll tell you

☐ **Sponge a child who has a high fever with alcohol.**
___True   _X_ False

Sponging a feverish child is certainly one means of reducing the fever. The liquid evaporating on the skin cools it, and in turn lowers the child's overall body temperature.

Alcohol as a sponging agent may work well. However, it is a poor and dangerous choice. Although alcohol is only absorbed in minuscule amounts through the skin, your child can inhale its vapors. Some cases of near-fatal coma have been reported after sponging with alcohol in poorly ventilated areas. Because of the danger of using alcohol, (Dr. Behrstock) recommends that parents sponge their children with tepid water ...

☐ **Never put an infant in front of the mirror during the first year of life.** ___True   _X_ False

... according to the proponents of this belief, children may become vain, or thieves, or even never learn to talk if they see their own image so young. Many primitive tribes believe that a mirror can actually steal a baby's soul ... no scientific evidence exists to substantiate any of (these). In fact, playing in front of the mirror can be an enjoyable, stimulating experience for babies. Let them look till their heart's content.

☐ **Children who begin walking earlier will be more intelligent than those who begin walking later.** ___True   _X_ False

The normal onset of walking can begin as early as eight months old, or as late as eighteen months. There is absolutely no correlation between the onset of what we call "gross motor skills" (like walking, sitting, and crawling) and either the child's future intelligence as measured by IQ tests or his or her future athletic prowess—as long as these basic motor skills begin within the normal ranges ...

☐ **Cutting a baby's hair weakens the infant.**
___True   _X_ False

This myth is probably (pardon the pun) "rooted" in the biblical story of Samson and Delilah. But there is no medical substantiation for the belief that cutting the hair effects a child's (or an adult's) strength.

☐ **Helping a baby stand too early can lead to bowlegs.**
      ___True   _X_ False

... this parental concern is goundless. Your child won't be harmed in any way. And, in fact, while in the standing position, the budding toddler will develop a sense of balance that will eventually be needed in order to stand unassisted and to walk.

☐ **Cold weather, chills, and wet feet cause colds.**
      ___True   _X_ False

In one public opinion poll, 64% of those surveyed believed that colds were caused by chilling. ... In reality, colds are caused by contact with people who have a cold—not by drafts, chills, wet weather, cool air temperature, or any similar environmental factor ...

☐ **Spinach will give your child added strength.**
      ___True   _X_ False

Although no one can deny that spinach provided Popeye with boundless vigor, its special mystical properties work only in the comic pages. ... Because spinach is extremely low in calories, it is a poor energy source, and even though it is rich in vitamins A, B, and C, these chemicals are present in many other foods as well.

So, while spinach is a fine food for your children to eat, it is not indispensable, as many parents believe, and is probably not worth the family battles that often occur when the kids refuse to eat it.

☐ **Teething can cause fever.**   ___True   _X_ False

... numerous studies reveal <u>no</u> connection between high fevers and teething. A low-grade temperature of <u>under</u> 100.4°F (38°C) is frequently seen in teething children, but such minimal elevations of temperature can also be experienced by healthy youngsters of all ages. No medical evidence exists to substantiate a correlation between teething and fevers greater than 100.4° (38°C) ... if your baby has a fever exceeding (this), do not attribute it to teething.

(Excerpted from *The Parent's When-Not-to-Worry Book*),
Barry Behrstock, M.D., Harper & Row, NY, 1981

T is for her tender touch . . . ever so grand

Ten Wonderful Things Grandmothers can do for their Grandchildren

1. **Love them** freely and honestly with no strings attached, always, and forever.

2. **Talk with them.**

3. **Listen to them.**

4. **Play with them** (at their level and at their pace—it's unbecoming to compete with a four year old).

5. **Compliment them.**

6. **Surprise them.**

7. **Indulge them,** occasionally (check with Mommy and Daddy).

8. **Respect them.**

9. **Inform them** about the things Mommy or Daddy did when they were young.

10. **Share with them** the history of their family.

U is for the happenings she'll bend to

Ten Horrible Things Grandmothers Can do to Their Children

1. Interfere in the raising of their grandchildren. ("Julie, when did you get your ears pierced?" "Oh, grandma took me!")

2. Give advice when not asked. ("Isn't it time Becky should take ballet, swimming, and piano lessons?")

3. Promise something without first consulting Mommy. ("Sure, we'd love to take you kids to Florida next Christmas!")

4. Criticize Mommy in front of the grandchildren. ("Honey, why are you giving the kids macaroni and cheese again? You know they don't like it!")

5. Stuff their grandchildren with candy and food. ("Johnny, you look green. What exactly did you eat at grandma's?")

6. Overindulge their grandchildren with gifts. ("Sally, where did you get that nine foot Snoopy, that eight foot Winnie-the-Pooh and that seven foot Annie?")

7. Demand "center stage". ("Mom, could you move over ... we'd really like to get some movies of the kids.")

8. Not follow the explicit instructions of Mommy. ("Mom, it's 7:15, I asked you to please have the kids home by 6.")

9. Foresake their children for their grandchildren. ("Honey, I know it's your birthday, but I did promise I'd take the kids to the circus.")

10. Forget to respect Mommy's right to privacy. ("Honey, I hope you don't mind, but dad and I were just in the neighborhood ...")

is for what every Grandma loves to do

Something magical happens when parents turn into grandparents. Their attitude changes from "money-doesn't-grow-on-trees" to spending it like it does.

Since gift giving continues to be a favorite pastime of grandmothers through the ages, here are a few **TCOM** suggestions.

Taking Care of Mommy's
Gift Giving Rules for Grandma

- Ask Mommy for suggestions: she should provide you with a list of the types of toys, books, and records she and/or baby would prefer.

- Surprises are thoughtful: however, they should be returnable to avoid ending up with four copies of Richard Scarry's **A, B, C Book.**

- Clothes: please don't buy the child's second year wardrobe the day after he is born. You can't predict how quickly the child will grow and you can easily miss a season.

- Give at appropriate times.

When Grandma Shouldn't Bring Gifts
for her Grandchildren

- Every time she visits!

- When she's feeling guilty for not spending time with her grandchildren.

- On other people's days (Mother's Day, Mommy's birthday, Mommy and Daddy's anniversary).

- When Mommy asks her not to.

- To guarantee that they'll come and spend the night.

- To "one up" the other grandparents.

- To make amends with Mommy through the grandchildren.

R is for reviews and raves and ratings

It's hugs and kisses time. Time to shift from how crazy grandma makes Mommy to how crazy Mommy is about Grandma.

The Grandma Test
"You know your baby's grandma's the best if ..."

1. **+5 kisses** Grandma calls Mommy on Monday and offers her services to babysit any night of the week.
+10 hugs If grandma only needs one hour notice.
+150 hugs If grandma insists on coming during the baby's dinner hour so Mommy and Daddy can get out earlier.
−10 kisses and −100 hugs If "any night" really means Tuesday or Thursday between 7:50 P.M. and 9:45 P.M.

2. **+5 kisses** Grandma is visiting with Mommy and the new baby. Suddenly, the baby begins projectile vomiting and screaming during her feeding hour. Mommy says that's what the baby always does.
+100 hugs If grandma lets Mommy handle the situation, helping whenever asked.
+15 kisses and +100 hugs If grandma mops up the floor, too.
−150 hugs If grandma panics, rushes to the phone, and calls Dr. Plotnick, grandpa, Daddy and Aunt Harriet.

3. **+5 kisses** Grandma asks Mommy and baby to go on a shopping spree.
   +50 hugs If grandma "pops for" a new outfit for the baby.
   +100 hugs If grandma "pops for" a new outfit for Mommy.
   −150 hugs If the only things grandma "pops for" is the parking.

4. **+5 kisses** Grandma babysits while Mommy gets her hair cut and does her weekly marketing.
   +200 hugs If Mommy returns home to find her house clean, the laundry done, and her favorite dinner in the oven.
   −10 kisses and −150 hugs If Mommy comes home to find grandma in the middle of a hot canasta game.

5. **+25 kisses** Grandma volunteers to stay with the kids while Mommy and Daddy take a holiday.
   +200 hugs If grandma manages to keep everything under control and the baby totally happy.
   +25 kisses and +200 hugs If grandma's also arranged two play groups, knitted three new outfits, and refinished Mommy's antique dresser.
   −500 hugs If Mommy returns home to find the fire department, five paramedics, and three neighbors all helping to revive grandma.

6. **+20 kisses** Once a week grandma devotes the day to Mommy and the kids. She does whatever she can so that Mommy can have the day off.
   +100 hugs If after five hours playing with both children, grandma puts the baby to sleep and bakes Sesame Street cookies with the four year old.
   −100 hugs If after five hours playing with both children, grandma falls asleep, leaving a "cookie monster" loose in the kitchen.

7. **+10 kisses** Grandma confesses that she's not comfortable with new babies, but she'd love to help babysit when the baby gets a "little older".
   −100 hugs If grandma's definition of a "little older" is 18 months from now.
   −400 hugs If grandma's definition of a "little older" is 18 years from now.

Add up grandma's kisses and hugs. If grandma's in the black, throw your arms around her and hug and kiss away. If grandma's in the red, give her a consolation kiss and hug and ask her to reread this chapter.

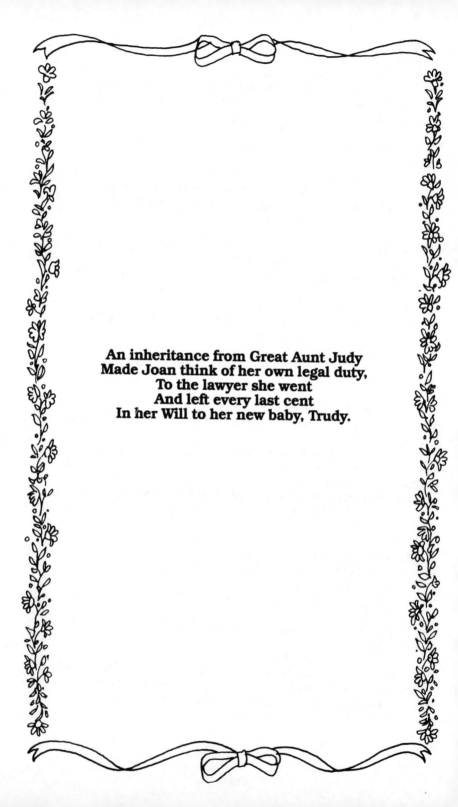

An inheritance from Great Aunt Judy
Made Joan think of her own legal duty,
To the lawyer she went
And left every last cent
In her Will to her new baby, Trudy.

The Legal Necessities

Things Over Which You Should Make a Federal Case

"What's the worst that can happen if I don't get my papers in order?"

"Nothing will happen to me ..."

"Oh, we don't have enough to worry about ..."

"Oh, we don't have enough money to pay for it ..."

"We have a family understanding. We don't need anything else ..."

"What difference does it make? Everything will go to my kids and my mother will take care of them ..."

"Yep. We're going to do it the first of the month. That's on the top of our list ..."

Lots of Mommies have lots of excuses for not getting their papers in order. They put this dreaded task in the same category as facing the dentist, the tax man, or the gynecologist (when not pregnant). However, when these three are avoided, the worst that can happen is a partial, an audit, or an empty Ortho dial-pack!

But put off drawing up wills, guardianships, medical authorizations, and insurance papers and the worst that can happen (if something should "happen" to you) is that your mother-in-law could raise your children, your divorced parents could be in a legal battle for 15 years leaving the children in limbo, or your husband could be forced to marry his college sweetheart.

So, for the sake of that "little munchkin" asleep in the nursery, take the time to make sure your children are well-protected with the assistance of a reputable attorney.

Where to find an Attorney

- Recommendations from family/friends
- Referrals from other attorneys
- State or local Bar Association referral service
- Legal clinics
- Phone directory yellow pages (expertise is often listed, along with fees for initial consultation)

Attorney's fees vary according to the services rendered. Comparison shop to make sure you're getting quality representation at a fair price.

(**TCOM Hint:** If you don't have a family attorney, begin with a general practitioner. If additional expertise is needed, he will advise you to seek co-counsel or direct you to a probate and estate specialist.)

Wills
"... and to my favorite niece, Louise ..."

While no Mommy denies her need for a strong will, she often denies her need for a legal will. Moreover, she is often intimidated by the legal process involved.

To ease the anxiety associated with obtaining this necessary document, **TCOM** presents a broad guideline to the standard provisions of a simple will.

(**TCOM Hint:** This is not a "Ten-Easy-Steps-To-Do-It-Yourself-and-Notarize-with-Your-Big-Bird-Stamp" Kit. Drawing up your own will (called a "holographic will") is not legally recognized in many states. Seek legal advice.)

Ten Articles Every Will Should Contain

1. Name and a.k.a. name (also known as).
   ("Mary Kathleen Thompson, a.k.a. Kati Thompson")
2. Provision revoking all prior wills and codicils (amendments), declaring this document to be the most recent.
   ("I hereby declare this to be my Last Will and Testament ...")
3. Provision stating all inheritance taxes, debts, and other outstanding obligations be taken care of first.
   ("I hereby declare my estate to settle up with Uncle Sam first ...")

4. Specific bequests: clearly describe the item to avoid discrepancy and identify the person to whom it goes.

("To my daughter, Mary Sue, I leave my three banded, gold wedding ring.")

Also, list any bequests to charity.

("To the American Heart Association, I leave the sum of $1,000.00.")

5. Beneficiaries: who shall receive the remainder of the estate and how shall it be divided?

("The remainder of my estate goes to my three daughters, Nancy, Joan, and Harriet to be divided equally.")

Note: Anything not specifically bequeathed is normally sold (liquidation of assets), unless heirs agree to other arrangements. ("You take the silver, you take the china, and I'll take the jewelry!")

6. Name an individual(s) to be the guardian and conservator of any minor children.

(An alternate should also be named should the original become unable or unwilling to act in the designated capacity.)

(Guardian): Has the care, custody, and control of the physical person of the minor.

(Conservator): Has the care and control of all real and personal property, including cash assets that are due to that minor once he becomes of age.

This can be the same person or two different people. (One person might be better with the kids, the other might be better with the "books".)

7. a) Name a "personal representative" of the estate and designate an alternate. (This is the new terminology for an "executor" or "executrix" in most states.)

The "p.r." is the person who accumulates, liquidates, and distributes the assets according to the provisions of the will. (He gives Mary Sue the wedding ring, the Heart Fund the $1,000.00, Nancy the silver, Joan the china, and Harriet the jewelry.)

b) Detail the powers and duties of the "personal representative", including a power of sale provision, which enables the "p.r." to sell real and personal property without a court order. (This allows greater freedom and flexibility for the heirs.)

(If Nancy, Joan, and Harriet decide they'd prefer "the cash", the "p.r." will thus have the power to immediately begin liquidation.)

8. The will must be signed and dated.

9. The will must be witnessed by at least two or three people, signed in the presence of each other and in the presence of the individual making the will.

10. Optional provisions: name an attorney to handle the estate (most simple wills do this) and include specific trust provisions.

Articles Every Will Should NOT Contain

- A list of safety deposit codes to "funny named" boxes.

- A list of trees in your backyard under which you buried the extra cash from "the business".

- A list of Swiss bank accounts with an up-to-date tally of their contents.

- A list of bequests to your "old flame" that exceeds the list of bequests to your spouse.

- A list of surprises to those you left behind, such as additional children your spouse knows nothing about. ("And to my beloved fourth daughter, Charlotte . . .")

Guardianship
"I hereby appoint my sister, Bertha . . ."

Considerations for a Great Guardian

- Someone who is warm and loving toward your children and makes them feel happy and secure.

- Someone who adores your children, like grandma, might be preferable over a younger aunt or uncle (despite her age).

- Someone who shares your values and beliefs, including religion, education, and lifestyle.

- Someone you trust to carry out your wishes, including providing your child with a stable home environment.

- Someone who has all of the above qualities, plus is a member of your family.

(**TCOM Hint:** Godparents are traditionally thought of in a guardianship role. If this is your desire, turn this honorary position into a legal one.)

TCOM Survey Results:

"Who are the legal guardians for your children?"

59% chose parents

20% chose siblings

14% haven't any

7% chose close friends

Medical Authorization
"I give my permission to Grandma to have Little Tommy sewn up if . . ."

(Check with your local hospital and pediatrician to specifically determine if any additional items should be included.)

Medical authorizations are used when parents leave their minor children in the temporary care of another individual. These authorizations are essential in an emergency situation when an instantaneous medical decision is necessary. The circumstances need not be "life threatening", but this document may save your child's life.

A complete medical authorization includes the information deemed appropriate by your doctor and attorney to assure its validity in your community. It should be drawn up by an attorney, or at least approved by an attorney, the hospital, and/or doctor.

(**TCOM Hint:** Update the medical authorization everytime you leave town, so that it is clear to all that this document is current.)

Articles Every Medical Authorization Should Include

☐ Name(s) of custodial parent(s), identifying them as such.

☐ Name(s) of minor children involved and ages.

☐ Name(s) of person(s) you are leaving in temporary care of minor(s) and that person's relationship to the minor(s).

☐ Your authority to the temporary custodian to give necessary medical permission to the doctor or hospital to treat the child.

(This can be in the form of a blanket authorization for all conceivable medical emergencies, or in the form of a limited authorization detailing specific situations.)

☐ Signature of the custodial parent(s), dated and notarized.

(Note: Most hospitals require a signed release provision holding them harmless from any decision the temporary custodian makes. This should be contained in the above medical authorization.)

Life Insurance
"And to my beloved wife, Dora, I leave a piece of the rock . . ."

Life insurance is typically carried by Daddy for the purposes of taking care of Mommy in his "absence". However, due to the increasing numbers of Mommies contributing to the family's income, many Mommies now have policies, too.

Ideally, life insurance guarantees the maintenance of a lifestyle to those left behind. There are two main types of life insurance for Mommy and Daddy to consider:

1. **Term:** lower in cost; you purchase a specific coverage for a fixed premium for a designated period of time (usually one year); guaranteed renewal at the end of contract, but the premium increases every year; no cash value; if you live you get nothing, if you die you get the face value of the policy. (Term insurance is similar to car insurance—you are paying for a service.)

2. **Whole Life:** higher in cost; you purchase a specific coverage for a fixed premium to stay in effect until death or maturity of the policy; builds cash value; the policy can be cashed in at any time for the accrued value it has earned; if you live long enough (maturity) it will pay the face value; if you die, you get the face value of the policy.

How to Get Out of Town Legally

• Have a current will drawn up reflecting all of your wishes.

• Make certain your will includes a designated legal guardian for your children.

• Prepare a medical authorization form to leave with the temporary custodian.

- Make sure you have adequate life insurance coverage, and that someone at home knows where all your important papers are. And finally . . .

- Thank your attorney for giving you peace of mind.

You Know You've Chosen the Wrong Attorney If . . .

1. All of his clients dress alike . . . two piece cotton black and white horizontal striped tops with matching bottoms.

2. You call his office to make an appointment and his four year old daughter confirms "Friday at three".

3. You inquire about the size of his legal fees and he inquires about the size of your savings account.

4. You give him top billing at your annual cocktail party and he gives you top billing at the end of the month.

5. He bills you for the times he spoke to you when you accidentally ran into him at the cleaners, the grocery store, and the movie theatre.

6. The esteemed members of his Bar Association include Jim Beam, Johnny Walker, and Jack Daniels.

7. The best "legal" advice he offers you is: 1 milk, ½ fruit, and 4 oz. sliced chicken.

8. You found his card (or his card found you) under your windshield wiper while you were parked at the Mercy Hospital Emergency entrance.

9. You inquire about his professional track record and he replies, "I'm down to a seven minute mile."

10. When asked which attorneys he holds in the highest regard, he replies, "Judge Joseph Wopner, Owen Marshall, and Perry Mason".

You Know You've Chosen the Right Attorney If . . .

- He's accomplished everything you've asked:
  - Your will is in order
  - Your children have legal guardians
  - Your two year old "Sluggo" is protected with a medical authorizational slip, should he slip when you're out of town
  - Your husband's been reminded to adequately insure himself

- He sets you at ease: you can reveal everything from the complete history of your savings account to why you're "saving" your children from the fate of Aunt Betty and Uncle Fred . . . without having to worry about reading it in the morning paper.

- He's known for his sharp mind, his good judgment, and his keen sense of fair play.
  (And, besides, he's married to your best friend.)

- His delivery service includes your completed will, your medical authorization, and a bucket of chicken and ribs.

Chapter Reference: Judge Joseph J. Pernick, Chief Judge Wayne County Probate Court, Detroit MI.

Though she dreaded a week's separation
Molly knew it was time for a vacation,
   When her husband inferred
   Bottles, burps and Big Bird
Were her main topics of conversation.

Busting Loose

The Great Getaway

Mommy and Daddy take a Holiday

You've settled into the routine. The novelty has worn off, the gifts have stopped coming in, and your mother-in-law's pop-in visits have become the highlight of your day. It sounds like you're ready for a vacation.

Whether you go across the street or across the state line, Mommy and Daddy must get away to get back:

- their sanity ("Can't we, just once, think of ourselves first and not the baby?")

- their sexuality ("Can't we, just once, think of ourselves first and not the baby?")

- their serenity ("Can't we, just once, think of ourselves first and not the baby?")

- their sleep ("Can't we, just once, think of ourselves first and not the baby?")

How does Mommy really know when it's time to take a holiday? Start by consulting the chart. If you can relate to six or more "ways", begin planning a getaway now.

"12 Ways You Know It's Time to Get Away"
(TCOM Survey Results)

"The First Half": Setting Priorities

Once Mommy and Daddy decide that they have the money, the time, and the sitter, the fun begins. ("You know, Harv, they say half the fun of taking a trip is planning it!")

Before you grab the luggage, ask the following questions:

☐ "How much can we afford to spend?"

☐ "How long can we afford to be away?"

☐ "Who can we afford to have stay with the baby?"

In the fury to get away, Mommy and Daddy may opt for the same trip their neighbors just took ("Sally and Bill raved for weeks") without stopping to think if it's right for them.

Or what's worse, Mommy and Daddy may each have private expectations about the trip without taking the time to share them with each other. If the thought of a vacation sends Mommy digging for last summer's white dress pumps and Daddy digging up the backyard for worms, somebody's going to be disappointed. (Unless there's a nightclub in the middle of the Chattahoochee River!)

Unrealistic expectations spoil more trips than anything else. To ensure the success of your first getaway after the baby's born, Mommy and Daddy should take the following test— *together.*

(**TCOM Hint:** Don't forget to comparison shop to get the most for your vacation dollars. Make sure you don't pay for "extras" that you are not going to use.)

The Great Getaway Test
—or—
What Mommy and Daddy Really Want Out of a Holiday

(Directions: Circle one description from each category, which best defines your concept of travelling.)

1. **"Rejuvenation"** is ...
   - ♡ a 15 hour sleep.
   - 🎾 15-Love.
   - 🐾 a 15 mile hike.

2. **"Deluxe accommodations"** are ...
   - ♡ Daddy showering first, so Mommy can sleep in.
   - 🎾 Daddy caddying, so Mommy can play another nine.
   - 🐾 Daddy in the stern, Mommy in the bow.

3. **"Privacy"** is ...
   - ♡ room service, rather than the coffee shop.
   - 🎾 singles, rather than doubles.
   - 🐾 kayaking, rather than canoeing.

4. **"Excitement"** is ...
   - ♡ Daddy coming out of the bathroom, smelling of Listerine and Old Spice.
   - 🎾 Daddy coming off the courts, smelling of a good workout and Ben Gay.
   - 🐾 Daddy coming into the tent, smelling of Pickerel and 6-12.

5. **"Peace and quiet"** is ...
   - ♡ the toilets flushing, the icemakers jingling and the bed springs creaking.
   - 🎾 the hush of the crowd, the beat of your heart and the woosh of the ball.
   - 🐾 the crickets chirping, the owls hooting and the wind rustling.

6. **"Fun time with Daddy"** is ...
   - ♡ spending the money Daddy just made.
   - 🎾 returning the ball Daddy just served.
   - 🐾 cooking the fish Daddy just caught.

7. **"Thirst quenchers"** are ...
   - ♡ Daddy.
   - 🎾 Gatorade.
   - 🐾 Smokey the Bear.

8. **"Great entertainment"** is ...
   - ♡ Daddy swinging from the chandelier.
   - 🎾 Daddy swinging the clubs.
   - 🐾 Daddy swinging from a vine.

9. **"Danger"** is ...
   ♡ running out of money on Fifth Avenue.
   🎾 receiving a pass from the cute tennis pro.
   ⇢ turning left when the tour guide turns right.

10. **"Haute cuisine"** is ...
    ♡ Steak Diane, flaming tableside.
    🎾 Weenies, rotating in the snack shop window.
    ⇢ Chili con Carne, simmering over an open fire.

11. **"Friendly natives"** means ...
    ♡ striking a bargain at Sunday's Flea Market.
    🎾 being asked by Betty-Lou, Barbara-Jean and Billie-Jo
       to complete their foursome.
    ⇢ waking up and finding the racoons left your breakfast
       intact.

12. A **"Scenic view"** is ...
    ♡ Daddy's tushy floating in a heart-shaped tub.
    🎾 Daddy flexing his muscles while jogging in place.
    ⇢ Daddy's hairy chest peeking through his red flannel
       shirt.

Scoring:

8-12   You're looking forward to a romantic holiday. You'll find
       it at the corner motel on a water bed or cruising on "The
       Love Boat". You'd like a few days alone with Daddy to
       renew your relationship. Good food, a bottle of wine
       and Daddy are all you need. You'll set the mood,
       regardless of the place, by bringing the stars and the
       moon with you.

8-12   You're looking forward to a sporting holiday. You'll find
       it at a camp, a clinic or a course in your own
       backyard or at any of the fine regional resorts around
       the country. You'd like a few days to unwind with Daddy
       at the spa or on the slopes. A round of tennis, a game
       of golf and Daddy are all you need. You'll set the mood,
       with the help of good weather, by bringing the clubs,
       your skis or the racquet with you.

8-12   You're looking forward to an adventurous holiday. You'll
       find it camping, climbing, or canoeing in your state's
       national park or on a guided wilderness tour. You'd like a
       few days to get back to Daddy by getting back to nature.
       A good life preserver, a spare set of oars, and Daddy
       are all you need. You'll set the mood, with the help of
       a roaring fire, by bringing the tent and the tackle box
       with you.

The Vacation Planners

Now you know what you and Daddy are looking for in a vacation. Consult one of the following to find the trip that's right for you.

Travel agent: They do more than just book flight arrangements. A good travel agent will work with you to define your options and help you get the most for your travel dollars.

Travel Section at the public library: (TCOM Recommendation: Stephen Birnbaum, **United States 1983,** Houghton, Mifflin Co., Boston, 1982)

Newsstand: Look in the classified advertising section in the back of special interest magazines – sailing, running, etc. – for terrific and inexpensive vacation ideas.

Newspaper: The travel section of your local newspaper features current information on holiday accomodations, prices and planning. The travel editor is also available by phone to answer additional questions.

Travel clubs: AAA and other motoring organizations.

Seven Great Ways to Fake a Getaway

1. **European Plan:** Turn your basement into a dream holiday with the help of colorful travel posters, authentic cuisine and your next door neighbor, Marge, who's just enrolled in a 10-week belly dancing course.

2. **The Overseas Plan:** Enjoy a delightful evening in Greektown. Drink the Oozo, close your eyes, and imagine you're in a far off land.

   (**TCOM Hint:** Make sure Marge isn't apprenticing at the restaurant you choose.)

3. **Weekend Plan A:** Swap houses with grandma. You get her four poster bed, her cat, Mimi, and a good night's sleep. Grandma gets your water bed, three month old Annie, and a 17-page list of "What to do in case of ..."

4. **Weekend Plan B:** Keep your own house and swap Annie for Mimi.

5. **American Plan:** Savour a fun filled day in your own home-town. Tour the art museum, the peanut butter factory, and the mayor's mansion. (This plan also includes pancakes at Uncle John's, "red hots" at the Coney Island, and fried clams at Hojo's.)

6. **One Night/Two Days Plan:** Check into the corner motel on Saturday morning and emerge on Sunday night.

   (TCOM Hint: Don't forget to take along the picnic basket, and the wine.)

7. **"An-Hour-Here-An-Hour-There" Plan:** Lose yourself in a good book.

You Know Your Getaway Was a Success if . . .

- You gained more than ten pounds

- You are still speaking to Daddy

- Daddy is still speaking to you

- You can still walk

- You had something else for breakfast besides apple-sauce and rice cereal

- You were able to break the automatic habit of waking at 2 A.M.

- You changed clothes because you wanted to, not because they were dirty

- Your tone of voice, which was previously two octaves above middle C, has returned to normal

- You called home less than three times per day

- The passion you felt for getting away is the same as the passion you now feel for returning home

Time Out for Mommy

When Mommy needs to get away mentally, but she can't leave the house physically, here are some suggestions based on **TCOM Survey Results.**

1. Fantasy Reading (Fiction)

Here's **Taking Care of Mommy's** reading list of "easy-to-pick-up, put-down-and-come-back-to" books ... fun fiction that offers Mommy a few moments or a few hours of delightful fantasy escape.

(**TCOM Note:** There are many outstanding books, which have been deliberately omitted from this list. They either don't fall into **TCOM's** "new Mommy reading" category or they are too well-known (like Harlequin and Silhouette romances). Once the baby is sleeping through the night and you've devoured the 16 titles below, you may be ready to move on to a "heavier" reading list. Consult your local librarian or bookstore owner for recommendations.)

A Woman of Substance, Barbara Taylor Bradford

Century, Fred Mustard Stuart

Chances, Jackie Collins

Class Reunion, Rona Jaffee

Compromising Positions, Susan Isaacs

Deceptions, Judith Michael

The Defector, Evelyn Anthony

Forever Amber, Kathleen Winsor

The Heart Listens, Helen Van Slyke

Mistral's Daughter, Judith Krantz

Portraits, Cynthia Freeman

The Princess Bride, William Goldman

There Should Have Been Castles, Herman Raucher

Rage of Angels, Sidney Sheldon

Rich Man, Poor Man, Irwin Shaw

Spring Moon, Bette Bao Lord

2. Factual Reading (Non-Fiction)

TCOM Survey Results:

1. Dr. Spock, **Baby and Child Care**
2. Frank Caplan, The Princeton Center for Infancy and Childhood Development, **The First Twelve Months**
3. **The Womanly Art of Breast Feeding,** Mary B. Carson, ed., La Leche League International

3. Fantasy Reading (Catalogues)

From ordering toasted macadamia nuts to toasting Evan Picone's new fall line, many Mommies are outfitting their homes and themselves via the catalogue via their bathtub. According to the Direct Mail Marketing Association in New York, one-fifth of American shoppers are participating in "the catalogue game".

Catalogues are fun to read, time saving, and best of all, a great way for Mommy to shop the stores from coast-to-coast. Browsing is generally free (sometimes there may be a nominal charge for the catalogue) and can be done at Mommy's convenience, since most stores now have a 24-hour hotline service.

Here's a terrific assortment of colorful catalogues featuring the latest fashions, housewares, indulgences, and gift-giving ideas for Mommy.

L. L. Bean (sporting and camping gear)
7641 Spruce St., Freeport, ME 04033

Bloomingdales (fashion/housewares)
Bloomingdales, NY, NY 10022

Childcraft (toys)
20 Kilmer Road, Edison, NJ 08818

Conrans (home furnishings/fashion)
145 Huguenot St., New Rochelle, NY 10801

Joan Cook (general merchandise)
3200 S.E. 14 Ave., Ft. Lauderdale, Fla. 33316

The Crate and Barrel (housewares)
195 Northfield Rd., Northfield, ILL. 60093

Gardener's Eden (gardening)
P.O. Box 7307, San Francisco, CA. 94120

Honeybee (fashion)
2745 Philmont Ave., Huntington Valley, PA 19006

Horchow (fashion)
P.O. Box 340257, Dallas, TX 75234

Lands End (sportswear)
Lands End Lane, Dodgeville, WI. 53595-0001

Williams Sonoma (kitchenware/gourmet cooking)
P.O. Box 7456, San Francisco, 94120

(**TCOM Hint:** In addition, many major department stores offer seasonal catalogues. Contact the store's customer service representative.)

IF— For Mommy

If you take time to fill your empty kitchen
   And fill your zealous mind before you're due,
If you take time to show Dad how to pitch in
   And help him understand the need for two;
If you take time to float in restful bubbles
   After a day in search of your layette,
If you take time to pack away your troubles
   And find a baby doc who does not fret:

If you take time to breathe with each contraction
   And focus all the while on "pink and blue",
If you take time to savour your reaction
   When noting that your son looks just like you;
If you take time to keep your spirits sailing
   And share with roommate—phone and lav and Sitz,
If you take time to keep guests from prevailing
   And save Day One at home for favorites:

If you take time to dance at whirlwind paces
   Yet, take a spin or two just for yourself,
If you take time to skip the ice cream places
   And tuck the nacho chips upon the shelf;
If you take time to seek the perfect sitter
   And show her how to put your mind at ease,
If you take time rekindling long-lost glitter
   By camping out with Dad though you may freeze:

If you take time to thank those thinking of you
   Yet, don't allow their thoughts to weigh you down,
If you take time to help a Grandma renew
   And fill in Big Bird for Bozo the Clown;
If you take time to pack each precious minute
   With Mommy's special love, yet hold in view,
Your need for space, fulfilling dreams, within it,
   Then you'll be **Taking Care of Mommy**, too!

(A grateful acknowledgement to Rudyard Kipling for inspiring us to write
this rendition of "If" for Mommy.)

Bibliography

Barber, Virginia, and Skaggs, Merrill Maguire. **The Mother Person.** New York: Bobbs-Merrill, 1977.

Benton, Barbara. **The Babysitter's Handbook.** New York: William Morrow and Co., 1981

Birnbaum, Steven. **United States 1983.** Boston: Houghton Mifflin Co., 1982.

Boston Women's Health Collective. **Our Bodies, Ourselves.** New York: Simon & Schuster, 1973.

Burck, Frances Wells. **Babysense.** New York: St. Martins Press, 1979.

Cardozo, Arlene Rossen. **Woman at Home.** Garden City, New York: Doubleday & Co., 1976.

Cherry, Sheldon H., M.D. **Understanding Pregnancy and Childbirth.** New York: Bantam Books, 1973.

Chirtok, Leon. **Motherhood and Personality.** Philadelphia: J. B. Lippincott Co., 1969.

Cooper, Mildred, and Cooper, Kenneth H., M.D., M.P.H. **Aerobics For Women.** New York: M. Evans and Co., 1972.

Curtis, Jean. **Working Mother.** Garden City, New York: Doubleday & Co., 1976.

DelliQuadri, Lyn, M.S.W., and Breckenridge, Kati, Ph.D. **Mother Care.** Los Angeles: J. P. Tarcher, Inc.

Deutsch, Helene. **Psychology of Women.** Vol. 2. New York: Bantam Books, 1973.

Dodson, Fitzhugh, Dr. **How to Father.** Los Angeles: Nash, 1974.

Dodson, Fitzhugh, Dr. **How to Grandparent.** New York: New American Library, 1981.

Heffner, Elaine, **Mothering: The Emotional Experience of Mothering After Freud and Feminism.** Garden City, N.Y.: Doubleday & Co., 1978.

Insel, Deborah. **After the Baby Is Born...Motherhood Your First 12 Months.** Washington, D.C.: Acropolis Books Ltd., 1982.

Karmel, Marjorie, **Thank You, Dr. Lamaze.** Garden City, N.Y.: Doubleday & Co., 1959.

Katch, Frank and McArdle, William. **Nutrition, Weight Control and Exercise.** Boston: Houghton Mifflin Co., 1977.

Kelly, Marguerite and Parsons, Elia. **Mother's Almanac.** Garden City, N. Y.: Doubleday & Co., 1975.

Kuntzleman, Charles T. and the Editors of **Consumer** Guide. **How to Choose The Exercise That Suits You Best.** New York: William Morrow & Co., 1978.

Lazarre, Jane. **The Mother Knot.** New York: McGraw-Hill, 1976.

Marzollo, Jean. **Nine Months, One Day, One Year.** Hagerstown, New York: Harper & Row, 1975.

Morton, Marcia Colman. **Pregnancy Notebook.** New York: Bantam Books, 1972.

Post, Elizabeth L. **The New Emily Post's Etiquette.** New York: Funk & Wagnalls, 1975.

Radl, Shirley L. **How to Be a Mother — and a Person, Too.** New York: Rawson Wade Publishers, 1979

Rich, Adrienne. **Of Woman Born: Motherhood as Experience and Institution.** New York: W. W. Norton & Co., 1976.

Thomas, Clayton L., M.D., M.P.H., Editor. **Taber's Cyclopedic Medical Dictionary.** F.A. Davis Co., Philadelphia, 1973.

Vanderbilt, Amy. **Amy Vanderbilt's Etiquette.** New York: Doubleday & Co., 1972.

Magazines

Brown, Diane Girard. "The Reproductive Revolution." **Monthly Detroit,** October, 1981.

Clarke-Stewart, Alison. "The Day-Care Child." **Parents,** September, 1982.

Editors of **American Baby.** "Labor and Delivery Guide." **American Baby,** October, 1982.

Farran, Dale. "Now for the Bad News." **Parents,** May, 1982.

Gillis, Phyllis. "Coping with Job Stress." **Parents,** April, 1982.

Isaacs, Susan. "All in a Day's Work: Four Women's Stories." **Parents,** May, 1982.

Tilling, Thomas. "Women & Money." **Parents,** May, 1982.

Yarrow, Lea. "How to Get Your Husband to Help." **Parents,** May, 1982.

Yarrow, Lea. "20 Questions About Birth and Delivery." **Parents,** January, 1982.

Paula Sherman Linden, R.D., is the mother of two and the former Chief of Dietetics at a metropolitan Detroit hospital. Susan Gross is the mother of one and an advertising creative consultant. Together they have developed a unique program for taking care of themselves, as well as their children. It's a formula based on strong common sense and an undying sense of humor.